"Sitaram Dass is a writer in the tradition of the great mystic poets: Kabir, Rumi, Hafiz, and the original Mirabai, and his use of language is infused with that divine spark. His poems awaken joy, which often is in short supply. His essays explore how the teachings of Ram Dass and Neemkaroli Baba relate to materialism, gender and race, and the delicate balance required in holding suffering, compassion, karma and grace in one life. I loved reading this book: as he says Ram Dass taught him, Sitaram Dass shows us an example of what is possible when we fully honor our human hearts."

—*Mirabai Bush, founding director of the Center for Contemplative Mind in Society and author of* Walking Each Other Home

"There is sweet wisdom here and deep devotion, and Ram Dass's love perfume that infuses SitaRam's words and heart, offered here to you."

—*Jack Kornfield, founder of Spirit Rock Meditation Center and author of* The Wise Heart

"In these luminous pages, Sitaram Dass embodies the teachings of his beloved mentor, Ram Dass. The warmth of devotion melts any meaningful distinction between cultivating loving awareness of the perfection of all that is and a wholehearted YES to alleviating suffering in the world, between art and activism, poetry and spiritual practice, between self as separate and Self as one with the One."

—*Mirabai Starr, author of* Wild Mercy *and* Caravan of No Despair

"In this beautiful book, Sitaram Dass sings his boundless love of serving Ram Dass and his guru, Maharaji, in sacred poetry and consecrated prose. You'll fall in love along with Sitaram—and for those of us blessed to spend time in the divine household on Maui, it all rings true. I'm inspired and touched by Sitaram's generous, courageous revealing of his heart's journey to God. I can feel the love and joy that suffuses it all. May you bathe in Sitaram's wisdom and compassion as you savor the learning he offers to our world."

—Trudy Goodman, founder of InsightLA

"In the many hours, days and weeks I shared with Sitaram Dass at Ram Dass's home on Maui, I was always deeply touched by his kindness, his sweetness, his intelligence, and his devotion. He is a relatively "young" man who embodies the wisdom, depth, and clear perception of a very old soul. His dedication to caring for Ram Dass was deeply touching. And it was abundantly clear how very much Ram Dass loved him... and enjoyed his Presence. This lovely collection of poems and writings emerged from Sitaram Dass's joyful, radiant Heart. They offer the reader a delicious taste of the unfolding of the Light on one Beautiful Soul's journey hOMe."

—Ramananda John E. Welshons, author of **One Soul, One Love, One Heart** *and* **When Prayers Aren't Answered**

From and for God

COLLECTED POETRY AND WRITINGS ON THE SPIRITUAL PATH

Sitaram Dass

The events and conversations in this book have been set down to the best of the author's ability, although some names and details have been changed to protect the privacy of individuals. Any stories related to author's service work with clients are made-up fictions based on amalgams of experiences from over a decade of work.

ISBN: 978-1-7355305-0-5 (Paperback)

ISBN: 978-1-7355305-1-2 (Ebook)

Library of Congress Control Number: 2021931995

Front cover and book design by Beverly Hsu

Edited by Pavan Das (M. Ceurvorst)

Forwards by Dassi Ma Kathleen Murphy and Krishna Prem (E. Bushnell)

First printing edition 2021

KRIPA
कृपा

Kripa Publishing
P.O. Box 4303, Arcata, CA, 95501

https://kripa.guru

I dedicate this book to the feet of the Guru,
Who is Neem Karoli Baba, Siddhi Ma, and Ram Dass,

One Being,
Eternally guiding the hearts of devotees

To a love within heartbreak,
A grace within grief,
A safety within death.

Guru Purnima, July 4th, 2020

The author donates 100% of his profits to Hanuman Maui,
a 501(c)3 nonprofit with a mission to preserve Ram Dass's
legacy on Maui and foster community through the teachings of
love, service and devotion.

Half of those proceeds are specifically designated for
Kripa's service projects through the Sacred Community
Project, a program under the direct fiscal sponsorship of
Hanuman Maui.

Kripa works to lower the barriers of access to contemplative
and devotional practices through affordable, free, and
donation-based offerings and prison outreach.

KRIPA
कृपा

https://kripa.guru
https://hanumanmaui.org

Contents

Foreword

It was my honor and responsibility to manage Ram Dass's household and affairs for the last 15 years of his life. He was my teacher for more than 25 years and the most important person in my world. He showed me what it means to live in Love.

During my time with Ram Dass I was privileged to share in the company of many wonderful people—from celebrities to spiritual teachers, Sitaram Dass always stood out as a deeply embodied soul who exemplifies service and devotion.

I witnessed Sitaram Dass's growth while serving his teacher with love and respect. During his time at the house he transformed from Ken Sandin to Sitaram Dass, the proverbial journey from role to soul.

I remember Sitaram Dass's impassioned letter to Ram Dass expressing his love and requesting a visit. I wondered if it was a whim of some young hippy only fascinated by Ram Dass's psychedelic experiences, but my initial concerns were quickly pacified upon witnessing their beautiful meeting. He asked Ram Dass if there was any work he could do around the property and shortly after the meeting Sitaram returned to Maui to stay.

Upon return he rented a little space in Paia and bought a wreck of a car that made more noise than any vehicle I had ever heard. He once offered me a ride in that car and I felt like I was in a tin can destined for doomsday. Fortunately the car didn't last very long...

Sitaram Dass enthusiastically worked in the gardens for several days a week and before long he moved into a jungle hut down the road. He cemented my love and admiration when I witnessed him arriving barefoot every morning after walking at least three miles along the highway to do his work here at the house. Ram Dass and I thoroughly enjoyed his company and soon asked him if he would like to move in as a full-time caregiver.

Once in the house Sitaram put up a tent in the backyard to use as space for sadhana. He spent almost every free moment in that tent singing to God. He would sing 108 Hanuman Chalisas for six to eight hours on his day off. His deep love and devotion for Ram Dass and Maharaji were vividly apparent.

When Sitaram was asked to do a chore he was always right on it, and you could rest assured that the task was done quickly and correctly. Once, a larger-than-life celebrity came to interview Ram Dass and I was overly determined to have the house looking spick-and-span. That was the only time that Sitaram balked at doing a chore. His resistance was a great teaching for me because he was demonstrating that we are all God and that there's no need to impress one person more than anyone else.

Sitaram Dass has dedicated his life to deepening his spiritual practice and sharing his path with others. He is a truly committed, dedicated, and selfless servant of the deepest character. I feel it was Maharaji's grace that Sitaram Dass arrived at the house to serve Ram Dass, and that river of grace continues to flow through the pages of this book.

From and for God reflects a deep spiritual journey. Sitaram Dass shares his path in a way that it is accessible and relatable to our own spiritual development. The wisdom available on every page of this book makes it a valuable account for any soul on the journey to awakening.

Dassi Ma Kathleen Murphy
President, Hanuman Maui
November 2020

Foreword

When I first landed on the island of Maui on July 24, 2012 to serve Ram Dass, I arrived late in the night. Someone was supposed to come pick me up and help me settle into these new and unfamiliar surroundings. I remember waiting for a moment, and then a white Ford pulled up to the curb and out jumped a barefooted being with a subtle grin, SitaRam Dass. My first impression was his unassuming nature. I thought "He seems unguarded, just like the pads of his feet." We began the long drive down a winding highway into the jungled side of the island, where Ram Dass lived. It's funny, I can still picture the glowing tracers left by cautionary markers and reflective paint perpetually passing, dissolving into my sight as we sped over the rolling hills. At the time however, I was completely blind in a way—I had absolutely no idea how deeply I would fall in love with my shoeless chauffeur.

As we arrived and unloaded, SitaRam asked if I was hungry. I said yes, as I had not eaten since leaving home much earlier that day. I was thinking, "Hmm... maybe we'll make a soup or we can have rice and beans or something like fresh fruit or..." when SitaRam just pulls out one single purple sweet potato, chops it up and puts it in a frying pan with oil. The Yelper in me scoffed... until I tried it. It was so good. So comforting, simple yet so colorful, nutritious and filling. Not surprisingly, these qualities are never far when I'm around or even drawn to think of my dear friend SitaRam.

During the period of transition, as I was coming into service at the Dass House and SitaRam was on his way out into the greater world, I began to pick up his deep sense of spirituality. I peeked into the small hut he had built on the land and saw a small altar table with pictures of saints, deities and some holy books. At the day's ending, SitaRam would often go and chant in this hut, and it seemed like he really wanted to be there instead of doing anything else. I began to notice that chanting was very important to him, and at the time I had no understanding of why, or what that was all about.

Similarly to the sweet potato though, that stagnant pondering only lasted until I tried it with a (tiny) shred of sincerity. Since then, the cultivation of my own chanting practice has been a main vehicle for me to express devotion and has drastically altered the way that I am in myself and how I move in the world. In this way, though we are equals I often see SitaRam as my teacher. Ram Dass showed me my infinite nature, bathing me in undying Unconditional Love; yet SitaRam was the first younger person that I found who is devoted to Maharaji, and in that, my first mirror of my true nature in a relative context. Really, SitaRam showed me the way to take care of Ram Dass and to move in the world with Maharaji enshrined in my heart— how do you ever repay a giving like that?

Since then SitaRam Dass has constantly inspired me in the direction of the devotional mood, leading me to study texts, learn prayers and rituals, host gatherings and create service projects. As we ripen together and grow closer, the love, the affection, and the truth between us simply increases. Over the years I have also gotten to witness the stream of his poetry and writings. I (like Ram Dass) do believe that writing is his Dharma, as reading his work has not only inspired my mind toward that Big Love, but kept me company when I suffer its absence.

In that same spirit, my recommendation to you would be to savor these fruit-pages. Rather than reading it like a "good business student," let yourself be comfortable; disarmed in a way. Go slowly as if you are peeling back the petals of a rose, gently exposing the next layer of fragrant mystery.

In this collection SitaRam has generously given us a mix of short poems and some essays, making this book a lovely exploration cover to cover. However, due to its style it is also a very enjoyable meander, leaving it open to more of a non-linear exploration. Read a poem before you run out the door to chase down the day's needs, sit and have tea with an essay, or perhaps bring it along to share with your friends. Either way, I am excited for you because when you read this book, you will understand why SitaRam Dass is my deepest friend and brother.

Yours in love,

Krishna Prem (Evan Bushnell)
Member of Kripa
May 2020

Introduction

My time with Ram Dass was the most meaningful in my life, as it set the foundation for everything that has come since. He has completely changed the way I think, the way I relate to my experiences, how I fill my time, where I place my value... My life can never be the same because of one man. I might get caught up in mundane matters and avoid my daily practices, but his influence is always present as a constant backdrop. He even brought me my closest friends and spiritual family. Ram Dass has touched every single aspect of my life, and there are no words to describe the kind of gratitude that comes from that. I owe him more than I can ever repay, and that is one of the ways that a true teacher shows us what Grace is.

How I got there all started with an idea and a simple yearning. At 23 years old, I realized that Ram Dass was the most influential person in my life, and I wanted to meet him. I told this to my friend Daniel, who instantly said, "We should just go to Maui and find him." We immediately researched and found round trip tickets from Seattle to Maui for $260. I didn't have much money, and that price was just right to make it a possibility. It was also a few hundred dollars cheaper than any other flight we saw. We told a third friend, Tyler, about this, and he said, "Two hundred and sixty dollars! We should just go right now!" We became completely caught up in the moment, and we bought the tickets on the spot.

Soon after, reality set in. We didn't know Ram Dass, and didn't even know anyone that knew him. We had no connection at all. Why we thought we could show up on Maui with no relationship (and no money) and somehow spend time with him was beyond any semblance of a rational thought.

So my anxiety started to set in, and I began exploring the ramdass.org website to see if there was some way to meet him. I discovered that Ram Dass did regular heart-to-hearts over Skype. So I emailed to ask if I could do my heart-to-heart in person.

I never heard a response, and it was all beginning to sound unrealistic. But something else started happening around that time. I began experiencing signs and synchronicities that made me feel that maybe it would work out. Some of them were small, like when I asked for the time off of work and learned that Ram Dass had a big influence on my boss. This gave me a little hit of hope, but doubt still persisted.

Other signs were more obvious. For the last few months I had been listening to Krishna Das obsessively and reading Ram Dass's book about his guru, *Miracle of Love: Stories About Neem Karoli Baba*. I had no idea that Krishna Das and Ram Dass knew each other or that they had the same guru. I also was having trouble believing the "bus story"[1] in *Miracle of Love*. Out of all the stories, I am not sure why I was so fixated on that one, but I just couldn't handle it. It's like it didn't have a place in my mind to land.

So when I watched the documentary about Ram Dass, *Fierce Grace*, and saw Krishna Das tell the bus story, my mind was completely blown. Not only did Krishna Das know Ram Dass and have the same guru, but they were on the same bus!

It's still hard to explain exactly what happened in that moment. Somehow, and I don't know how, but I just *knew* that I was going to meet Ram Dass. After the movie ended, I looked up Krishna Das's tour schedule and discovered that he was coming to Seattle the day *before* we were already set to leave for Maui. I took this as a sign. It was *my* bus story. Greater forces had conspired even before I "decided" to buy my plane ticket.

Feeling much more secure, I wrote another email to the foundation. This time I did receive a response.

"Ram Dass keeps a rather aggressive schedule and attempts to meet the many requests that come his way. One of us will be back in touch with you before the weekend about the schedule."

It wasn't a yes, but it was enough. I just *knew*.

A few weeks later I went to the Krishna Das concert, and that was actually the day that inspired me to buy my first harmonium and begin my chanting practice. The next day, Monday, June 8th of 2009, my two friends and I flew to Maui. We hitchhiked and slept on a beach in Paia until I got the call from Dassi Ma.

Ram Dass was so gracious to us, listening to all of our stories and answering our questions. As I laid out my story, and all of the ways that my path winded me to him, he simply said, "Well, you know, no one comes before me unless Maharajji[2] sent them."

I had no idea what that meant, but I knew in my heart that it felt *right*. During that meeting, Ram Dass said that if I was on island, "there might be something you could do to help." Well, that was enough for me. I returned home, and for the next three months I saved up all the money I could, quit my job, and moved to Maui. I paid someone a hundred dollars a month in rent to sleep on their back porch and use their kitchen and bathroom. Dassi Ma,[3] Ram Dass's primary caregiver and Ma of the house, invited me over to work in the garden, and I thought I was volunteering. I worked for three hours, and then she paid me and said I could come back the next day. Wow!!! I was Ram Dass's gardener! I thought I had won the lottery.

Two months later, I moved onto a permaculture farm that was three miles away from Ram Dass's house. It was just close enough that I didn't need a car, and I would wake up before sunrise, eat my breakfast and walk along the Hana Highway while doing japa on the mala beads that Ram Dass had given me to arrive at their house by 8am to work.

On the permaculture farm I did work trade to live in a small, eight-foot-diameter bamboo hut with no electricity. Dassi Ma lent me every single book they had about this mysterious "Maharajji" that Ram Dass was referring to. With little distractions or comforts, I had ample time to read spiritual texts, develop my chanting practice, and to write. The first poem in this collection was written shortly after I moved into my little bamboo home.

After a few months of working in the garden they invited me to move into the house to serve full time. It was my deepest heart's wish come true, and I was beginning to believe Ram Dass's words.

About This Book

This book is a selection from my collected writings and poetry over the last decade. It is my attempt to apply Ram Dass's teachings to my spiritual path and all of the complexities, horrors, and beauties of living in this modern world.

The poems were, for the most part, all written during the three years I was on Maui with Ram Dass and Dassi Ma. Ram Dass once told me, "Writing is your dharma," and I took that to heart. On my days off I would sometimes go to a local coffee shop and devote my entire day to crafting even one simple poem. It was as if poetry served as a liminal bridge that could grant glimpses of the Wordless through words, and it was a way for me to process what was happening during this profound and transformative period of my life.

My time with Ram Dass provided me with the protection needed so I could begin to ripen into my spiritual path. Besides living with and serving my teacher and becoming immersed in an amazing spiritual community, I also didn't have to pay for rent, car insurance, food, or any other expense. Everything was taken care of.

And then, three years after I moved to Maui, I met my current life partner and left the island. Although I knew in my heart it was the right thing to do, it was still a heartbreaking decision. And life got hard for a while. I was no longer protected, and at 27 years old I realized I didn't really have any work experience or marketable skills. I went from living in paradise with my teacher to working three different minimum wage jobs in Los Angeles and trying to figure out what it meant to be in a serious relationship.

It was around this time that a shift happened, and I began writing in prose. My mind was grappling with the complexities of what it meant to live a spiritual life in this modern world as I attempted to apply Ram Dass's teachings to my relationships, work, suffering, and my growing understanding of the ways that power, privilege, and oppression operate in society.

It wasn't until recently that I began writing poetry again, and I attribute this to my newfound friendship and brotherhood in Kripa.[4] The only two poems that were not written while in Hawaii, "Wail-Moans" and "SītāRām," came out of directly being in their presence.

Whereas the first poem in this collection was written shortly after moving to Maui to be with Ram Dass, the book ends with what I wrote the night that Ram Dass left his body. This was done to give a narrative arc, but the writings are not in any chronological order.

The name for this collection, *From and for God*, has two inspirations. The first is a line by J.D. Salinger:[5] "I mean, all she was doing was pouring God into God, if you know what I mean." This line was most likely drawn from the Brahmārpaṇam, a sloka from the Bhagavad Gita[6] that is often recited before meals and is the second inspiration for this title:

Brahmārpaṇam Brahma Havir
BrahmāgnauBrahmañāhutaṃ
Brahmaiva Tena Gantavyam
BrahmakarmāSamādhinah

Brahman[7] is the offering, Brahman is the oblation
Poured out by Brahman into the fire of Brahman,
Brahman is to be attained by him
Who always sees Brahman

From and for God is also the name for the first self-printed book of poetry that I gave to Ram Dass. I printed it from Kinko's and stapled the binding by hand before handing it to him. Many of those first poems are in this collection. In that way, I see this as a blossoming of the first seeds that I handed to him over 10 years ago.

From and for God is an acknowledgment that these are my attempts to titrate the Formless Ineffable into tangible words as an offering to God. This is an impossible task, but one that I relish in. My mind may try to co-opt these into its own narcissistic gratification, but in truth any yearning for God must in fact come from God, and any creation that comes from that yearning must come from the same Source. It is both an aspiration and a way to give credit where it is due. Of course, any imperfections (of which I am sure there are many) are from my own flaws, and I take responsibility for them. And how beautiful is that? That God can speak to us through imperfect means? That is the greatness of the Beloved, that They use imperfections to remind us that They are in fact... everywhere.

Many of these writings can be found on my blog, and the Be Here Now Network has published two of them on their own website. The Wholistic Heartbeat has reprinted two of my writings in their quarterly magazine, and some of my writings are also present in two different book anthologies that will be coming out soon.

A Note on Language

I use the terms Maharajji and Neem Karoli Baba[8] interchangeably, and his name is sprinkled throughout these writings. He is a deep part of my own worldview, and anytime I wrestle with spiritual teachings and try to apply them to my life or the world, His presence is a central part of that. He is the guru of my spiritual lineage and the mirror of the God within. He is the Great Siddha[9] that forever changed Ram Dass's life in 1967. Through Ram Dass, Maharajji made his way to the West, and it has never been the same since. Maharajji doesn't care about receiving credit, but his influence ranges from spiritual teachers to lawyers, judges, non-profits, the tech industry, public health... at this point we have no idea just how profoundly Maharajji has weaved himself into the fabric of western culture. This was probably stated best by a man in prison at San Quentin, who said to our band Kripa while we were there for a kirtan, "Maharajji has infiltrated the West, don't you think?"

Even though the audience for many of these writings was my own spiritual community, I hope that they can be meaningful to anyone who picks up this book. For this reason, I have tried to use accessible language whenever possible and provided endnotes when using less common terms. I also used endnotes for certain Sanskrit terms to write them in IAST[10] standard form and have provided a glossary with a basic pronunciation guide at the end. If this is something that interests you, I strongly recommend finding a teacher that can help you get started with the intricate and thrilling path of learning Sanskrit.[11]

On Pronouns and Capitalization

I have had a long habit of interchanging capitalized male and female pronouns when describing God in the abstract personal sense, even sometimes using a capitalized "It" to describe God's impersonal aspect. In Sanskrit, for instance, the word for the impersonal, transcendent God is Brahman. Brahman is a neuter noun. Thus, per the Sanskrit rules, "It" is an appropriate pronoun to use in these situations.

It should be known, however, that there is no capitalization in Sanskrit. Capitalizing pronouns out of respect when referring to the Divine is specifically something that has grown out of the Judo-Christian tradition. It is a form of respect that I have grown to appreciate and love. Beyond this, capitalization is something that I have found I can play with in my writing, allowing me to use many poetic names to refer to that Eternal, Ineffable Love.

In the last five years, however, I have also begun using a capitalized, singular "They." Not only does "They" honor the plurality of gender identifications and expressions, but it is also a more accurate use of language to reflect the concept of God. I have heard feedback that interchanging these pronouns can be confusing to some readers, and thus to clear this confusion, I am writing this to explain the reasons, intention and aim for this.

Grammatically speaking, the singular "they" is now almost-universally accepted and is recommended from groups ranging from Merriam-Webster to the Associated Press. A short summary of the reasons why runs along these lines:

It has existed in the English language for at least several hundred years in both casual and formal speech as a gender-neutral pronoun. The "rule" against it is rather new, overly rigid, and tedious. English has always been an evolving language, and there is no reason for this to stop now. As we return to a more fluid understanding of gender in mainstream, western society, we need to move beyond the gender binary in our language.

In Hinduism, God is described in multitudes of ways and is commonly referred to as being nonbinary. There is Brahman, the aspect of God that is impersonal and genderless, but there are also personal forms of God that are beyond the gender binary as well.

For instance, Lakshmi[12] is often referred to as the feminine form of God and Narayana[13] is often referred to as the masculine form. However, even these forms are beyond gender. And, in reality, Lakshmi and Narayana are not separate. Lakshmi-Narayana is one being, the Underlying Essence of Reality, simply referred to in English as God. Lakshmi-Narayana is beyond anything that our mind can conceive of.

Besides the genderless, transcendent and personal aspect of the Divine, God can take myriad forms depending on a devotee's needs. This includes a wide set of relationship roles including Master, Parent, Friend, and Lover. It also includes the entire gender spectrum. Not only can God manifest as He or She, but gender-fluid, nonbinary, androgynous and intersex representations of Divinity have existed in India, Europe, and throughout the world.

Thus, the singular, capitalized, "They," functions in multiple ways.[14] It points to the genderless, transcendent aspect of God while also signifying that God can be feminine, masculine, both or neither. It is a more accurate pronoun to describe the Ineffable, and its use points us towards a more fluid and liberated understanding of gender. If God really did create humanity in Their image, then as we move towards accepting a broader range of gender identity and expression in society, we also move towards a deeper and more expansive understanding of God.

POETRY

Starlight

I am in one of those moods again
where I just want to kiss
anything that moves.

I would even kiss the Sun
if he would let me, but instead
he has climbed down
his own sunbeam
and nestled in my heart.

Now, when I kiss the plants,
the insects, or the Moon,
they burn
into stars.

This is what you
are yearning for, dear lover.
Just lean closer, and let me
kiss you
into who

you really are.

Splendor

The gods and saints
never stopped showering us with flowers.

We have just forgotten
how to walk on this earth
lightly

as if every step
pressed into a petal
to release its sweet
fragrance.

Yes

Can we be bonded by a faith like this?
where our own existence
is enough? and our faults
seem to vanish
in its ocean of magnificence
the way a mosquito
seems to vanish
as it dances
across the sun?

This *here we are*
    is the gateway
into a Love
    so abundant
that ripe plums
    weigh their branches
to hover above
    our cupped hands.

I may have reasons for doubt,
but those plums... so deliciously full, so ready
to burst! ...they seem to say
yes.

True Conversion

True conversion
is not the swapping of words,
the trading of dogma
or the switching of casings
that harden the heart.

It is when the shells shatter
from a swelled heart blossoming
that we are truly born again.

Wail-Moans for Love Scraps

The poets press their faces to the Love-Room's door,
begging for scraps from *that* Love Affair.

One of them catches a love-drunk whiff and cries out:

> Raaadhaaaaaaaaaaaaa! Krishnaaaaaaaaaaaaa!

(It's as if you can crawl inside of that sound
   and melt
 into electrified longing...)

I will tell you, the philosophers aren't even inside of that house;
they hand out leaflets on the street corner
and debate the meaning of muffled sounds:

> Is it One? Or is it Two?
> Are the waves separate from the sea?

But there's no riddle to unlock; no Sphinx guards the gate.
It swings open, wildly
on the winds of the lover's cry,

and some of those leaflets actually say to go in!
I even saw one that said:

> Become a drunk poet
> and wail-moan
> for Love scraps.

Addiction

What I most want to do tonight
is wrestle the sky, grab
a good-sized
chunk
and wring it like a
wet rag
for a single drop
of light.

Fragility

Let me touch my
lips to your cheek, so
I may swallow your tears.

Then, maybe
they will enter my bloodstream,
and I can finally feel
your preciousness
with my entire
body.

Mustard Seed

This is the faith
found folded inside
the absence
of all things,

existing
not for god
or for man or the angels
but for its own
Existence.

It's what's left
when loss and confusion
have stripped away the nail
from where the universe
hangs.

On Beauty and Sorrow

Soothing rains can only fill
as deep as the shovel digs.

Paradise is an island of beauty
with winds of sorrow and bliss.

Even quilts weaved
from spiders and rainbows
will rot when covering mold.

But mold unmasked
is sorrow felt deeply,
waking the heart of the soul.

Butterfly

Taste your sorrows
the way a caterpillar
sinks her feet in the mud—
each of the leg hairs tremble
as they lick the wet, savory
earth.

Music

No true poet
claims to create beauty;
they discover it
the way a tambura player
discovers
that perfect place on the string
to stroke.

Deep within your soul
there is an antique table
where the two Buddhas, Sorrow and Joy,
sit to have tea.

Their arms rest on the table's edges
as they lean close to each other's eyes.

Within their intensity
lies four golden strings
waiting
to be played.

Don't Worry

Don't Worry,
this pain you are feeling
is nothing more than
the excruciating agony
of two holes drilled in your back
and wings shoved in.

Wings

An unharvested tree will only produce rot.
Even a goddess will sour if trapped in a box.
Tonight my back aches
from the weight of wings
unused.

I Guess They Call This Writer's Block

I can hear the river's call
dancing along the bank.
It is the very sound of Life
as it pours from the heart.

This Stream of Silence
carries no passengers-
no stones, fish, or debris,
only water
flowing.

Yes,
I feel inspired, and yet
the pen rests on the page
in Stillness.

How many ways are there
to say, "I Love You?"

This Time

This time
　　let me be open—
no bait, no traps, no clever
schemes, no hooks or ropes...
The moon doesn't try
to lasso the sun, for she knows
her ropes will burn. Instead
she basks in the light.
　　With open arms
I will wait.

Mantra

I tried to be a saint once; it didn't
work. So now I carry
a pocketful of zippers
when I walk into town.

I lay them on the sidewalk
and pull on their sliders, separating
the concrete to reveal

the sweet mystery of light and sound
that bounces between bamboo
stalks when played upon
by the wind.

Release

What would be left of you
for me
if I no longer wanted
you
to be a something
else?

Afterthought

...it is Thank You
and I Love You, it is Joy and it is
Yes! it is the rising sun revealing
a soft pair of hands
sprinkling salt on the
snow-covered
sidewalk.

Autumn's Cry

A leaf lightens
into gold
and leaps
from the branch to the sky.

What whirling what spinning what dancing what joy!

(It is jealousy that clings
the other leaves to their branches, but only
for so long.)

Autumn knows this secret—
that we are all becoming beautiful
together.

The Way the Earth is Lit

I have heard it was said
by them of old time
that the Moon
borrows her light
from the Sun.

But I say
a beauty as great as the Moon's
inspires a great lover,
and it was this muse
that sparked the Sun's flame.

The Sun's sweet ballads
of love and longing
share the Moon
with all of us, and
in that sharing we are

given hope
that we too can find
such a Beauty
to ignite us
into existence.

Collapsing the Distance

This is what *Thank You* means—
it is when the pores become
      so wide
that the wind
can slip through the skin
and tickle the heart.

It is acceptance
with Love.

And it draws our surroundings
closer—the chair, the ocean,
the trees... it brings them
inside.

It holds the atoms in my body
together, and now holds
your atoms
to mine.

Intimacy

I see a bright crescent
forming like a smile
at the bottom of your
pupil. (This is how pain
condenses to
honey.)

I unwrap the wool from
my body and allow
this thick nectar
to soak

through my skin.

SītāRām

The way "Seeeee" stretches the lips to a smile,
how "Taaaaaa" drops the jaw, and the eyebrows
raise in delight.

We often think of ecstasy as the pinnacle of pleasure,
but it's really a fierce melt
into horror
and bliss.

And that's just one moment
in the river of sound, "Raaaaaaaaaa;"
its alluring current swallows and dissolves.

The Merciful Nature is revealed
when despair dawns at the river's end—
an aching heart softened
by a low, soothing rumble,
"Mmmmmmmm..."

Maharajji gave me faith, unveiled
Unyielding Grace. Ram Dass
opened the Bottomless Well
of the human heart.

And SītāRām provides the perfect Form
to contain it all—

Faith, Grace & Love—

a sonic murti, formed
by my own lips,
by whose feet I fall
with the breath's rising tide.

SītāRām,
sometimes I think You're a practice,
but in truth
You're the reward.

ESSAYS

This Love Has Room for Our Protest

Without even noticing it, the conversation evaporated into silence. Ram Dass simply looked at me, and I melted into the chair, filled with love. I looked across the room towards him, and our eyes met. Just a few minutes ago he had told me the story of when Maharajji instructed him to meditate like Christ. Ram Dass asked him how Christ meditated, and Maharajji said, "He was lost in a sea of love."

I was absolutely head-over-heels in love with the man before me, not because he was Ram Dass, but because his presence pulled me into a depth of Being within that could love *anything*. I realized that this is what it meant, at least in some small way, to meditate like Christ.

Ram Dass often said things like, "I love the wall, and the carpet, and this chair. I love my wheelchair."

And when he said it, he meant it. I saw this, not just in my darshan with him that day, but during the following two years that I lived with him. I would often see him sitting by himself, not reading, or napping, or thinking, or even meditating, but just sitting there, truly present and content. Because of his stroke, he was confined to a wheelchair, and his body was often in extreme pain. Yet, he had a lightness about him that transcended his physical body. There was a joy and contentment that could be at home with the pain. As he approached his death and his body continued to deteriorate, that light within only brightened.

Some of my fondest memories are of driving him to his various appointments. I would try to make him laugh, or he would crack me up with his great sense of humor, but most of the time was spent in silence. With Ram Dass, this silence was not an awkward void to be filled but a rich delicacy to be savored. Once, while sitting on his back porch, he broke the silence to say, "See *this*? Don't you *see*? Look how beautiful it is..." He waved his hand across the scene in front of us, caressing the scenery with his fingertips and painting each tree, shrub, and cloud with the stroke of his hand while exhaling a long and slow, *"Ahhhhhhhh...."*

I saw it in the eyes of the guests who came to do private retreats with him. They too knew what it meant to be lost in the ocean of love, and I learned from them just how contagious this is. Ram Dass made a splash in them so large that its ripples could be felt in my own body, and I benefited just from their smiles. I went to almost every talk that Ram Dass gave, and I can't remember how many times I heard him say, "Bhakti[15] [love] is spread from one soul to another. Those who don't have it catch it from those who do."

I experienced this same thing with Siddhi Ma, a saint from India who, just from sitting in the same room as me, not even looking my way or giving me the slightest acknowledgment, could wash waves of love over me as if she herself was the gravity of the moon.

Of course, Ram Dass and Siddhi Ma both have pointed me, like all of us from our satsang, towards Maharajji, a perfect form of this Love. He is the sun that lights the moon. He is the gravity that holds all things in their perfect place, and he is the True Self within every heart.

Maybe twenty minutes or so had passed before Ram Dass spoke the next words. They were very slow and deliberate.

"You are Jesus and Maharajji," he said.

"So are you," I answered.

At that moment I knew the truth of what we were saying. I immediately remembered the words from *Be Here Now*: "This is Buddha meeting Buddha. Over toast and coffee. Over milk and porridge. Over mu tea and brown rice."

Because Ram Dass rested so deeply in his heart, it pulled me right into mine. He showed me a possibility, and he also left me with a practice—to see everyone as Jesus and Maharajji, to see them as God. *"For those with the eyes to see..."* It is truly possible to love everyone. That's what he has taught me and what I keep trying to return to.

Sometimes God will surprise me and remove one of Her many disguises, and then it's as if the lighting softens, revealing the most beautiful person to ever walk the face of the earth...

Sometimes it is a youth I am working with, who is screaming at me, calling me a *fucking idiot* for minutes on end... or an angry teen that is much larger and stronger than I am, could knock me out with one punch if he wanted to, and is telling me he wants to bash my face into the wall... or the grocery clerk for a moment when our eyes meet and the world stops...

Ram Dass kept a picture of Donald Trump on his altar, and this was not a cop-out. He wasn't approving or condoning. He was loving the most difficult person he knew of to love. This is not a spiritual-bypassing or an attempt to normalize a monster. It is the ocean, and it has room for all things, including Donald Trump. It doesn't mean we don't protest, of course we do. We fight for truth and justice and peace. Christ not only sought forgiveness for those who crucified him, he also threw the money changers out of the temple.

During that meeting Ram Dass told me to study the Bhagavad Gita. Since then I keep returning to its ancient words, and it constantly shows me its timely relevance. The Bhagavad Gita invites us to protest as if the universe depends on it while doing it as an offering to God, and this includes God in the form of Trump.

The way you offer love to someone who is screaming at you is to remain calm and not react. Expressing love in any other way, even the slightest smile, would not be appropriate or well received. The way you show love to the oppressed is to fight alongside them for justice. The way you offer love to an oppressor is to tirelessly fight their oppression.

But, for it to be a true offering our hearts must remain open. An open heart provides the courage to act with strength and the gentleness to act without cruelty. It creatively finds the path of least resistance that will do the most good. Whereas anger burns hot and fizzles fast, love is a long-lasting fuel that can keep us warm through even our burnout and despair.

> *The message you communicate with another human being has nothing to do with what you say. It has nothing to do with the look on the musculature of your face. It's much deeper than that. Much deeper! It's the vibrations that emanate from you!*
>
> —Ram Dass, *Be Here Now*

I have spent time working in group homes for young kids who experienced severe trauma in their lives. My experience showed that it was easy for staff to love the kids. It was so clear that the children's behaviors were not their fault. A violent youth was physically beaten by a step-father. A sexually-aggressive child had themselves been sexually abused for years.

But the understanding for the kids often did not extend to their parents. In fact, staff would often express vitriolic anger towards them. And isn't it reasonable to feel that way towards someone that could be so cruel to an innocent child? Yet, when looking through case files, I would often find histories of trauma that could go back generations. A father who had abused his son had also been abused when he was a child. A perpetrator of sexual abuse once lived in a group home just like the one I was working in. It dawned on me that these adults were once children, and I took a moment to imagine what it would be like to learn that one of the kids I worked with grew up to perpetuate the same harm they had survived. At what point could I say that it is now their fault? At what age does cause and effect become minimized? Not that I would ever condone any atrocity that one person commits against another, but if a kid I had worked with grew up to commit a terrible act, how could I not feel for them and weep?

Do what you do with another person, but never put him out of your heart.
      –Neem Karoli Baba (paraphrasing the poet Kabir)[16]

That's what Maharajji said. This is a guidepost, a statement of what is possible, and also a path to walk. We can act in this world, working for justice, peace, and the end of all oppression, and still never keep anyone out of our hearts.

This is not a poetry to soothe broken hearts that cannot hold the weight of the world. This is a deeper weight to tear the last pulsing seams apart. When we can fully drown in the world's pain, we are ready for its love.

This love has room for our protest. In fact, it demands it.

Beliefs Masquerading as Truth

Truth is that which can stand on its own. It needs no support. There is no amount of evidence or reasoning that can either prove or disprove Truth. We often call this type of knowing faith.

But there is quite a bit of confusion about faith. Faith comes from the heart. It cannot be found in the mind. This misunderstanding has pushed many into increasingly blind, rigid, and unhealthy viewpoints. By taking a thought and clinging to it against all evidence and reason, it traps us in the prison of our own limited perspective.

It cuts off all possibility for healthy discussion. It makes many feel that their religion is the only one and blindly leads millions to challenge the findings of science. This has made many agnostics and atheists skeptical of the role of faith in today's world.

Faith is not a belief that we hold to tightly. When our beliefs are misplaced as faith, we feel the need to squeeze them, as if we are trying to compress a fleeting sand into a solid rock. This squeezing may create the illusion of solidity, but it requires effort to continue the charade. The second we stop holding, it crumbles.

Faith requires none of that. It takes no energy or holding. Truth just is. It is found through the continual letting go of clinging in the mind. Truth is always present, but we can see it more clearly when our mind is open and free from clinging.

Truth is who we are. Faith is the inner knowing that comes from relaxing into the Truth of our Being.

To varying degrees, those of us on the path have faith. But we also have a whole stew of beliefs that have cleverly attached themselves to that faith. These beliefs stem from our own attachments, aversions, fears, insecurities, and cultural conditioning. So, though it's important to acknowledge our faith, it's also important to recognize our infallibility. Though we have contact with Truth, we don't fully understand what it means or how it relates to our life. And we don't always see it clearly.

At age 27, I left Ram Dass's home on Maui to travel to India with Jamie, my current life partner who I had recently met and fallen in love with. When Jamie and I returned from India, life seemed very difficult. I had left my "spiritual" life on Maui where I lived with my teacher, Ram Dass, and now I was in a "worldly" relationship with my girlfriend and living in L.A.!

It seemed to me I was running from my spiritual path and turning away from the deep faith I knew to be true. I was confused and screaming on the inside. I had totally lost my center, and I was certain of what I had to do to get it back. I was so sure of it that I almost left everything behind to run to Taos, New Mexico to live at the Neem Karoli Baba Ashram. I had contacted the ashram manager, bought a bus ticket and packed my bags.

On the day of my departure, Jamie was about to drive me to the bus station. Before we pulled away, she said, "I feel like this is a cop-out. I just feel like you are running away because life is hard right now." There are many other words she said that I don't remember. But from the moment she began speaking, I felt my heart begin to crack.

Before she could even finish her words, I completely broke down and began sobbing. It was a full-body cry, exploding from the heart as wailed tears. I hadn't cried that hard in years. I didn't even know I was capable of it.

I realized that she was right. My fear of commitment, my fear of having to find a job and pay bills... it all got the best of me. I hadn't worked a real job or had to worry about paying rent in years. I had never really been in a long-term relationship. I was scared. I just wanted to run away from all of it. This fear had masked itself in the cloak of "spirituality" by making the Taos Temple my escape.

I had misplaced my beliefs and understanding about my faith as the faith itself. And I clung to it tightly to stave off my gnawing fear.

When our life seems to crumble, when it seems that God is no longer with us, when it seems that we have lost our center, there is a great opportunity in those moments to enter into a deeper and more profound faith.

I have faith in Love. Love is who we are, it is the Ultimate Truth, and the fabric of Existence. I have faith in our Eternal Nature, in the Guru, and the path. I have faith that no matter what life presents to me, I am always safe. I am safe in Eternity. I am held in the arms of Love. I am eternally resting in the palm of the Guru's uplifting hand.

But I don't know what any of that means. I may think I do, and I may even be right, but the ideas I hold in my mind are beliefs that are either correctly or incorrectly aligned with ineffable Truth. And beliefs need to be open to inspection if they are to evolve and stay relevant. If they are to point us beyond the intellect and beyond belief, they need to be used lightly and not squeezed into substitutions for Truth.

I may be safe, but I could die tomorrow. Love is who I am, but I will continue to create karma for myself and suffering for others. The Guru may be with us, but this doesn't mean that we won't destroy the planet or that we are safe from another holocaust. It will be a long and tiresome fight if we are to progress as a species.

Though I know that compassion is the only answer and though I have access to Truth, it is filtered through my own limited experience and clouded by my attachments. I could be wrong about everything in my life, in politics, and in the world.

When I see myself holding on to a spiritual idea, this is the time for reflection. Why am I holding on? What am I afraid would happen if I let go? What deeper Truth could I find?

What Do You Want?

He asked if I could feel my heartbeat in my fingernails. "Take three more slow, deep breaths," he said. Then he asked if I could feel it in the front of my teeth.

I lifted a slight smile as my heart pulsed in my mouth like a subtle toothache. Now I was ready for the question.

"Sitaram... What do you want?"

A simple question, but deceivingly direct, like a garden shovel we overlook as it hangs in the garage.

I answered with whatever truth I could muster in the moment, probably something vague about Love or God, and then he asked again.

"Sitaram... What do you want?"

This same question was repeated, again and again, until my habitual answers had been fully spent, leaving me without the safety net of a pre-programmed response. A wake of anticipatory silence flooded the room as I waited for the emergence of a yet-unknown answer.

With each round of questioning, tension shed from my body as it sank into the soft couch of the transpersonal therapist's office. I had come seeking guidance as I tried to navigate my confusion over my relationship, my decision to go back to school, and my conflicting desires for how to be in the world.

Much of my spiritual life has involved "dropping out." I spent my senior year in college eating psychedelics and reading spiritual texts, and I almost didn't graduate. From there, I traveled to India, lived out of my car in the desert of New Mexico, lived with anarchists in a tree sit in Berkeley, dumpster dove for food in Seattle, and lived in a bamboo hut without electricity in the rain-forest of Hawaii. My first time having a bed in three years was when I moved in to serve my teacher, Ram Dass.

Shortly after leaving Ram Dass's home and starting a relationship with my current partner, I freaked out and almost dropped everything to live at the Ashram in Taos, New Mexico.[17] I thought I had worked through that, but now, several years later, it felt as if I still had two conflicting paths—*Do I leave behind everything, move into a van, and live as an American sadhu? Or... Do I stay in my relationship, keep paying the bills, and go back to school to get my Master in Social Work?*

In truth, it wasn't an either/or situation; my path has been a long, slow struggle to realize my freedom lies in my commitment. But the fear of surrendering to my Dharma—in the form of both my commitment to social justice and my relationship with my partner—scared the shit out of me.

The question, "What do you want?" cut through my neurosis and showed me that, underneath my fear and anxiety, there lied a deep trust in my path. My heart knew its next steps; I just needed a little help filtering out the noise.

There are no rules for how the heart unfolds. Rules are in the mind, often stemming from embedded cultural programs, deep wounds, and old stories. But the heart knows what it wants. It intimately understands its path towards freedom. One simple question, "What do you want?" unlocks a vast potential the mind will never understand.

Since that day, I have participated in the same exercise in a variety of group contexts, and each time it took on new meaning, always leading me towards the ever-unfolding intelligence of the moment.

I have also facilitated and asked this question when counseling friends, clients, seekers of Truth, and lovers of God as they navigate life's waters with the often murky compass of the heart. On more than one occasion,

I was asked if the question can be rephrased. Something about the word *want* hits a nerve, and instead they want it changed to something like "what feels right?"

I understand the reasons for it—we are on a path of letting go of desire, and it can seem on the surface like this is about chasing more of it. But it has been my experience that this is not the case, and by changing the question we dilute its potency.

What do you want is ownership. Accountability. Trust in our deepest self. *What feels right* makes it seem as if it is coming from somewhere else, as if what we are supposed to do is somehow different than what we want. It skips over an important piece: *Why?*

Why does it feel right?

I have come to the conclusion that it feels right because, underneath societal expectations and cultural programmings, shoulds and should-nots, old stories, past traumas, and our addictions to comfort and pleasure, this is what our heart yearns for.

What do you want is a deep trust in our own Being, the realization that what we want, what we *really* want, is to heal, to live to our full potential, to use our gifts to serve others, to relieve suffering and inspire joy, to plumb the depths of our heart and sing and dance for God, to live out our simple Dharma with reverence for all of life...

Our deepest wants are what God wants for us. Our deepest wants are what feels right. It feels right because our heart sings a resounding YES!

Deep down, at our core, we recognize that we can live a better way. We know we are not living to our highest potential, that the systemic violence of separation and exploitation—of racism, sexism, classism, ableism, imperialism, colonialism, and the destruction of our planet—are not what we want. We don't *want* this.

We are so addicted to maximizing pleasure and minimizing discomfort that we have misplaced these addictions as distorted forms of our deepest heartsong. We forget that this addiction is a response to a collective trauma that long ago left us feeling like we can't actually trust ourselves. We have forgotten that we are actually, at our core, *good*. This leaves us so disconnected that we are left frantically searching for ways to manage this dysfunctional system. But our methods only reinforce the illusion of separation.

Imagine riding a broken bicycle. The handle bars might fall off any minute, so you have to hold them tight as you turn. The pedals are jammed, and you have to press at a certain speed to keep them going—too slow and they won't move, too fast and they will freeze. The brakes don't work, so you are vigilant for pedestrians and cars while constantly scanning for creative ways to stop. It's not safe to ride, but you have places to go, it's the only bike you know, and everyone else is riding broken bicycles too.

We have grown highly skilled at riding our bicycles. It took years to get this good at it, and as our bikes continue to malfunction, we develop new skills to keep the ride going. But none of this prepares us for learning to ride a bicycle that actually works. None of our skills to minimize danger and harm will work on the new bicycle. We are so attached to our way of riding and so scared of something new that we ignore the heart's whispers about a new bicycle that is much safer and more fun. This is the predicament we are in.

We live in a materialistic culture that values individual pleasure above all else. We live out an old story that proclaims humans are at their core evil, nasty and brutish. The only option for us to live together, then, is to curb our deepest desires through fear and punishment. We have lived this way for so long that we don't even need an external authority anymore to police us. We do it to ourselves. So when we are asked the question, "What do you want?" we tense up to protect our broken bicycle from falling apart.

The fear is that this question will manifest as more narcissism and validate the exploitative and consumer values of our culture.

It has been my experience that the opposite is true. When we share our desires and allow them to be seen, the power of bringing our shadows into the light reflects for us that deeper want—buried for years under layers of guilt, shame, repression, and addiction—that knows our service is our greatest Joy. It burns away the work we do out of inadequacy so we have the space to do God's work, the work we *want* to do—Love, Serve, Honor the Sacred, Remember God, Tell the Truth.

On the devotional path, our primary means of letting go of lesser attachments is to remember that what we *really* want is God. It is said that the Gopis of Vrindavan are the gurus of knowing what to want. Their heart burned for Krishna and their last impurities were incinerated by the intensity of that yearning.

The lesser desires of the mind and senses only pull us away from our inherent Divinity and decrease overall satisfaction. As we grow on the path, instead of grabbing for illusive pleasures that cause discord, we begin to turn towards the wisdom of the heart, nourishing everyone, including ourselves. This is what we *want!*

The only danger is if we stop asking. Our addictions and cultural programmings run deep, and we need to always be careful of the ways these double agents can co-opt our deepest heart-song into instruments of separation. Each time we find our truest answer, we need to be willing to ask again.... and again.... and again....

so... since we're here...

What do you want?

Mistaking Individualism for Freedom

In today's rapidly changing society, many of us no longer want to work for others. We want to use our talents, creativity, and passions to develop our own business or work freelance. We no longer are willing to tolerate repetitive tasks, 40-hour work weeks or corporate bosses.

But it would be a mistake to think that this is breaking free of society, that we can remove ourselves from it, that we are somehow above it, or that we are trying to do something different. In truth we are only swapping forced conformity for a self-imposed one, and we mistake this individualism for freedom without acknowledging its paramount importance in the hierarchical value system of our society. We now turn the cog of culture at our own pace and rhythm, but we still don't question where the machine is taking us.

It is only privilege that creates the illusion of separation. Unless we acknowledge this, we are stuck in a mire of arrogance and indifference. We too are complicit in a system of exploitation that is ruining our planet and destroying entire cultures. Even with our artisan candles and organic coffee. Even with our job as a yoga teacher or a freelance artist.

The more I sit with this, the more I am convinced that analyzing the value systems of our culture and the ways it has infiltrated our most intimate desires, beliefs, and values is one of the most radical and deeply spiritual acts of our time. It is crucial for any real development, not because we can break free of culture, but because it is necessary if we are truly going to do our part to help change its direction.

It will take all of us if it is going to even budge an inch. This is one area where we can't rely on our leaders. Those holding power in our culture are often the ones most conditioned by it. But, if we all begin to question our own opinions, beliefs, desires, and values, even the so-called "spiritual ones," and question where the source lies, we may begin to awaken the collective mind into something deeper and whole.

Contemplative practices and time in satsang[18] can help give us the leverage needed to be critical of our mind, but I am convinced that this alone is not enough. A critical questioning must become its own form of practice. Meditation, yoga and prayer can actually strengthen and reinforce these cultural values, and all of us in our spiritual community are blinded by this cultural force. Not only do we help each other to wake up, but we also blind each other from our deep conditioning.

Questioning our culture and our privilege must be a part of the spiritual life. It will deepen our time in practice and enrich our spiritual community. It will lead us towards freedom, not an individualistic one, but a freedom of abundance that spills out to all corners of the world.

The Dharma of Our Times

I have spent years trying to find that morally superior stance that could acquit me of the suffering of society. As a young environmental and human rights activist I found solace by making corporations the enemy. They were the cause of our suffering. Eventually that no longer worked, and so I had to find another strategy. As I moved away from activism and towards a deeper sense of spirituality and alternative living, the goal became to remove myself from the system. Yet, no matter how much I gave up, how much I shopped at co-ops, drove gas made from veggie oil, or moved onto an off-the-grid eco village, I couldn't escape it. One day it dawned on me that even if it was possible to be totally off the grid, totally unreliant on any fossil fuel or system of government, totally in a sustainable way, I would still be responsible. It would require me to be completely removed and isolated from society while knowing what was going on. And how could I sit by idly while others were suffering? Wouldn't my lack of engagement still hold me responsible?

The world is a messy place. Global warming, habitat loss, and pollution are destroying the planet. Our corporations are run by greed, and we have corruption at every level of government. We are constantly bombarded by signs telling us we are not good enough and pushing us to buy more. Our world is in a perpetual trance of war, and we are inundated with systemic oppression and human-caused suffering at every turn.

And there is no perfect solution to make it all go away or to absolve us of this. This doesn't mean we don't try. We should still work to end suffering and to live life in a way that is in harmony with our values. But forming an identity from this weakens our effectiveness. It actually pushes the world away as we run into the safety of our labels and self-identifications.

The immensity of our global situation leaves us coping with strategies to keep it at bay. Some of us develop scapegoats, some of us ignore it through entertainment or our own personal concerns. Some of us try to escape through spirituality or alternative living. Some of us convince ourselves it's not really a problem, or even if we admit it is, we don't fully acknowledge it for fear that we will drown in a sea of unbearable guilt, fear, sadness and rage.

> We block it out because it hurts, because it is frightening, and most of all because we do not understand it and consider it to be a dysfunction, an aberration, a sign of personal weakness. As a society we are caught between a sense of impending apocalypse and the fear of acknowledging it. In this "caught" place, our responses are blocked and confused.
> –Joanna Macy, "Working Through Environmental Despair"

It feels like this giant quagmire, a ball of tangled knots that can't possibly be undone. Just to look at it feels exhausting. But it requires we look, for we are not standing from afar. We are in the middle of this knotted mess and interwoven in its very strands. Not acknowledging this prevents us from acting skillfully, and not acting is a form of action. It also has repercussions that send out ripples of cause and effect. It makes us a dead weight that adds burden to this already complicated tangle.

In the Bhagavad Gita,[19] Krishna tells Arjuna:

> Not by merely abstaining from actions can one achieve freedom, nor by renunciation alone can one attain perfection.
>
> Indeed, no one, even in the twinkling of an eye, ever exists without performing action. Everyone is forced to act helplessly according to the impulses born of the modes of material nature. (3:4-5) [20]

Arjuna desperately wanted to shirk his duties. He was ready to live as a renunciate. Faced against an army of friends and relatives in a war that could have no clear winner, with death and destruction for all guaranteed, Krishna's advice seems shocking:

Go and fight!

Why? Because it was his Dharma.[21] Arjuna was not able to prevent the war from happening and could not stop it. If he left, it would ensure the loss of the Pandavas, the force of goodness. There would still be death and destruction. Family members and friends would still kill each other. Arjuna's refusal to fight would actually create more suffering because the Kauravas would win, and righteousness would leave the land.

The Bhagavad Gita begs us to own up to our circumstance, as awful and complicated and no-win as it may seem, and to be engaged.

We are Arjuna in a no-win war. By acknowledging this we can embrace complexity. We can look at this from all sides, consider our own strengths and passions, as well as the needs around us, and do the needed work that the moment truly calls for.

This is Dharma. It's messy. The Mahabharata does not end happily, but with a society in ruins. Yet there was less suffering because Arjuna lived out his Dharma. He didn't run away to be a monk. He faced the seemingly-impossible riddle of his time and found the knots that were his to untie.

This has strong parallels to our current climate crisis. Most climate scientists tell us that it is already too late to stop the effects of global warming. We have already caused irreversible havoc to the planet and those already marginalized by society will be the ones to suffer most.[22] Habitat loss is happening at incredible rates, and it is estimated that 30-50% of all species could be extinct by mid century.[23] We are in a situation where looking at the bright side of things is actually harmful. And yet, still they urge us to act.

> *We must do something braver than try to save the world we have known.*
> *We must accept the fact that the world we have known is going to change*
> *in hideous and damaging ways—and we must nonetheless work as hard*
> *as we can to limit that damage, and keep it this side of complete catastro-*
> *phe, to save as many options for our descendants as possible. This, as*
> *I say, is hard... Once something's spoiled, it's easier to throw up your*
> *hands and walk away, which will be a great temptation for all of us.*
> *Still, we need to try.*
>
> —Bill McKibben, founder of 350.org[24]

Living in a Democracy is exhausting. Living in this technological age is exhausting. *Living* is exhausting. It has always been exhausting.

> *Now this, monks, is the noble truth of suffering: birth is suffering, aging*
> *is suffering, illness is suffering, death is suffering; union with what is dis-*
> *pleasing is suffering; separation from what is pleasing is suffering; not*
> *to get what one wants is suffering; in brief, the five aggregates subject to*
> *clinging are suffering.*
>
> —Buddha, *Dhammacakkappavattana Sutta*

There is nothing we can do to absolve ourselves of this. This is our burden to carry. Pilate may have washed his hands, but history holds him accountable.

It's impossible to not get involved. We are already involved. Realizing this is important, for the world needs us. It needs us to untie the knots, not for any reward or gain or to ease our own suffering, but simply because there is nothing else to do. It's not about holding a stance or political view, or joining a subculture or movement. It's not about creating new labels for ourselves. It's not about becoming *somebody*.

It's about letting go of our rigid stances and softening the boundaries of self, so we can truly see what is called for in the moment and act.

This is Dharma.

Where, then, does despair fit in? Why is our pain for the world so import-
ant? Because these responses manifest our interconnectedness. Our
feelings of social and planetary distress serve as a doorway to systemic
social consciousness. To use another metaphor, they are like a "shadow
limb." Just as an amputee continues to feel twinges in the severed limb, so
in a sense do we experience, in anguish for homeless people or hunted
whales, pain that belongs to a separated part of our body—a larger body
than we thought we had, unbounded by our skin.

—Joanna Macy, "Working Through Environmental Despair"

Intuition
The Wisdom of the Heart

Sometimes writing is like tunneling a hole into a rock with the slow, torturous drip of water. Other times it is a sculptor patiently inviting a wooden log to reveal its hidden shape. Today it is a sailor lost at sea when unexpected winds hit, and I jump from my slumber to raise the sails.

This is an apt way to start this piece, for the topic is intuition, or the trust in our own deepest wisdom. As far as I can tell at this stage of the journey, it is all we have.

Fierce and liberating, it is this Groundlessness of Being I am referring to, the realization that there is no external authority, nothing solid to cling to. I may seek guidance from wise teachers, counselors, and experts, look to peer-reviewed journals, follow the scientific method, or surrender to a Sacred Text or Guru, but it is the Still, Small Voice within that leads the way.

I am not claiming that we are each separate islands, as Carl Rogers[25] once claimed. This, too, grew out of his own trust in his intuition, but it was formed at a time before we suspected individualism's invisible hold on our thinking.

I don't believe there is some "me" that is separate from "you." Though our wells may appear to be different, we are drawing from the same Source. Rather than build bridges between islands, I see my work as dissolving the illusion of walls.

But I don't blame Rogers for this mistake. I have found that my intuition is always better in retrospect and constantly clouded by the invisible programming of dominant discourse.[26]

Luckily for me, this trust in my deepest wisdom is self-correcting. The deeper we dig, both individually and as a culture, the more we uncover unconsciously borrowed beliefs, oppressive power structures, ego defenses, distorted thinking, and the Reservoir of Pristine Wisdom underneath. I compare my findings to yours, we both make adjustments, and this shared knowledge benefits us all.

My experience has taught me that, right now as I write this, I am wrong about things I cannot yet even fathom. This confusion can often cause harm, and I acknowledge I am causing pain in ways I as of yet don't know.

Part of me wants to scream out to an authority to fix this. But where to turn? What criteria would I use to pick a leader or method, and how would I evaluate the criteria? How would I rate the evaluation?

When Krishna Das had to leave India, he asked Neem Karoli Baba, "How can I serve you in America?" Maharajji's answer was to repeat the question back to him, "How will you serve me in America?" That's when he heard the answer arise from his own heart. "I will sing to you in America."

This is what is often misunderstood by those who do not have a Guru, or who live outside of a faith or spiritual worldview. My relationship with my Guru, with my Faith, and with Spirit, is not a supplanting of my deepest Wisdom, it is an outpouring of it. My Intuitive Heart has led me to my spiritual path, and this path deepens my relationship with the Inner Well. As I grow in wisdom, my need to be convinced falls away, and I find myself naturally drawn to my practices, teachers, and sacred texts. It's just what feels right.

The same is true about trusting experts and peer-reviewed evidence. It seems much of today's revolt against specialized knowledge stems from a lack of trust of each other. Yet, I find that trusting in shared knowledge and community experts has only sharpened my intuitive capabilities.

An atheist or materialist may feel that a spiritual seeker has yet to develop a mature intellect. A spiritual seeker may feel that a materialist has yet to go deep enough into their own heart.

Both are just where they are at on the journey, each trusting their intuition to the best of their capacity. At various times in my life, I have found myself on both of materialism's sides. As I grow on the path, I watch as these seemingly disparate worldviews melt away into a deeper, Ineffable Essence. I trust this process will continue.

In the meantime, rather than building bridges, I will continue dissolving walls, and I aim to live my life in accordance with this Reservoir of Interrelated Being.

Radical Unknowing

Radical unknowing: the recognition that in each moment all we have to guide us is our own intuitive heart, and yet there is no way to ever know where each step will land, whether it will lead us towards our destination, or whether our destination is even where we want to go.

I am reminded of the autobiographical poem, "Berryman," by W.S. Merwin. In it, a young Merwin asks his poetry teacher how he can ever know if his work is "any good at all." His teacher responds:

> *you can't you can never be sure*
> *you die without knowing*
> *whether anything you wrote was any good*
> *if you have to be sure don't write*

Imagine you are walking through an unlit tunnel. It's pitch black, and you can't see your own hand inches away from your nose. You reach down and grab hold of a handrail. Your hand glides along the cold steel, offering a sense of comfort as you warily make your way through the dark... Until you feel your hand slide off the end.

The rail just stops. Panic sets in as you reach your arms to the side and realize that there are no walls anywhere near you. You aren't even sure anymore if you are in a tunnel or a giant cavern stretching out as wide as your imagination. You don't have any rails to rely on, but you also recognize something even more terrifying: the rail you were using up until now was never connected to a clear path. The sense of security you once felt disappears into the abyss.

A dear friend recently told me that he didn't like the word intuition. "I think its meaning has been diluted," he said. I can relate to this. We often see it as some sort of character trait that we possess, a super power immune from the checks and balances of logic, reason, and evidence.

Where I live in the rural redwoods of Northern California, there is a community member who is convinced that certain drum rhythms, especially the rhythms used in reggae, hip hop, and pop music, are of a "lower" vibration. Because he is so "sensitive" and "intuitive," he can feel his energy drain just being around these sounds, and he has even gotten sick from it. I once told him that I did not have the same experience that he did, and his response was that I was not evolved enough to notice. (He claimed it was because I am an "intellectual.") He proselytizes others so they too can awaken to these rhythms' disharmonious nature. For him, ridding the world of this evil sound is a key part of achieving world peace.

This may seem like an extreme example, but I think many of us do this in less obvious ways. In my counseling work with people, I have found that a major obstacle to receiving new information is when an "intuitive person" has access to otherworldly knowledge.

When someone "knows" something, it shuts off the possibility of being wrong. This is true regardless of where the information comes from, but "intuitive" knowledge often seems especially immune from correction. Instead of shaping and redirecting our inner compass to better fit reality, we create a list of justifications and beliefs to maintain our intuitive identity. This creates a mental wall that keeps us trapped in our own projections, imaginations, thought constructs, and isolated worlds. We stop listening.

But intuition is not a character trait. It is an *act*—the act of listening. We can't listen when we know. Listening comes from a radical *un*knowing. When I am with another person or a group, it doesn't matter if I am teaching, leading kirtan, or counseling, my goal is to let go of everything I know and listen. If an intuitive realization comes, I have two choices:

Option one: I retreat into my mind by developing that intuitive hit into an entire storyline. I am no longer listening, and I am not in tune. If I choose to believe my new "theory," then I can easily find evidence to justify it. Confirmation bias helps build up my mental construct so large that I lose touch with the actual territory of the moment.

Option two: I keep listening. There is an intuitive hit, and so I lean into curiosity. I check in. "I am wondering about..." This asking becomes another way to listen, as I take another sip from the relational moment. It doesn't matter if my intuitive hit was right or not. Either way, the response serves to help me tune in more deeply. More information surfaces, and my being is calibrated to a deeper listening.

Sometimes this information is as subtle as the tone and quality of a voice, a shift in a chair, or the tension or softness in a face, all of which requires a deep listening to notice. And then there are times where we are so in tune that suprarational information seems to come from no known cue at all. As long as we keep tuning, listening, and engaging in radical unknowing, we are deepening our capacity to draw from the moment's bottomless well of wisdom.

But as soon as we "know," we are in trouble. As soon as "intuition" becomes a character trait that we possess rather than a process of attunement, it acts as a barrier to listening.

Intuition is the moment-by-moment stepping into the darkness of radical unknowing.

The Nectar of the Name
A Story About Kirtan, Lila, and the Hanuman Chalisa

People don't know—every line of the Hanuman Chalisa is a Maha Mantra.

–Neem Karoli Baba

Many of us have come to kirtan and felt inspired, felt our sorrows lifted, or even experienced a deep healing or surrender. These are beautiful experiences that are meant to be cherished, but they are also ultimately just initial doorways into a rich and satisfying journey to God. Kirtan is more than just a temporary experience or emotional high. It is an opportunity to gain a taste of the nectar of devotion.

Just like in any worldly relationship, we first feel an attraction to someone, and some "high" in our body tells us we like them. If this initial attraction turns into a relationship, then over the years it has the opportunity to deepen into something even more satisfying than we could initially imagine. It has the possibility of offering an incredible healing and deeper sense of safety in the world. If this is true for a worldly relationship, then what to say of a Divine one?

What if our Lover was Perfect? What if They had no desires of Their own, save maybe for us to attain liberation? What if this Lover lived in our own heart as our True Nature? What if falling in Love with Them meant falling in Love with everyone, including ourselves? What if this Love affair fostered a sense of safety that stayed with us? Even through our most difficult times? Even through sickness, old age, and death? This is what kirtan can offer us—a chance to gain a taste of this nectar and to deepen this Holy Relationship.

I remember when Krishna Das recommended that I chant 108 Hanuman Chalisas.[27] I had only been living at Ram Dass's house for a few months, and I had only been singing the Chalisa as a practice for about a year. I was obsessed with chanting. I would go to every kirtan I could and would often volunteer to help set up at kirtan events. I had built a make-shift temple out of tarps at the edge of Ram Dass's property so I could chant whenever my duties permitted and not disturb anyone. When I chanted, it was like the heavens parted. All of my daily worries floated away as an upwelling of joy permeated my being.

"You do it on a Tuesday... you light a candle... you don't have to sing all of 'em; you can read some... And you can take bathroom and coffee breaks."

That was the extent of my instruction.

I was given one day off a week from my duties at the house, so I decided to make my next break on a Tuesday (Hanuman's day). I sang (and read) my 108 Chalisas, taking a few breaks as I had been instructed. It took about eight hours total. The experience was not exactly what I had imagined, though. Somehow I thought that, because a two-hour kirtan blasted me to the moon, chanting all day would annihilate me in the sun. Instead, I found myself battling boredom, exhaustion and fatigue.

The next day Krishna Das called the house to talk to Ram Dass. At that point, Krishna Das did not call the house on a regular basis, and it was not common for me to pick up the phone. When Dassi Ma was home, she usually answered it. So, when I answered the phone to hear Krishna Das, it was obvious the phone call was meant for me, even if I was not his intended audience. In the two years I lived at the house, I believe that was the only time I picked up the phone to find Krishna Das on the line.

"I sang 108 Hanuman Chalisas yesterday."

"Oh... How did it go?" he asked.

"It was good... I started to get tired... and kind of bored at parts," I sheepishly admitted.

"*Good,*" he said. "It's not about feeling some way or another. It's just about doing the practice. These practices work in the background. We want the immediate hit, but this is a system that works on us throughout lifetimes."

I was caught, and I knew it. Although theoretically I understood that the practice was not about achieving a "high," my day-long chanting ritual showed me where I was still attached.

"It doesn't seem like an accident that you are calling right now," I said. "It's kind of weird that you are calling the day after I sang 108 Chalisas for the first time."

"It's not an accident at all. And it is not strange either. This is how Maharajji works."

It was clear that I needed to spend more time with this practice. I decided to continue it on the next three Tuesdays, watching my mind go through the ups and downs of ecstasy, impatience, frustration, and boredom. In between these Tuesday sessions I strengthened my resolve towards my daily practice. I had recently begun reading the Ramcharitmanas, or the Tulsidas Ramayana, at the instructions of K.K. Sah, an elder devotee who had grown up knowing Maharajji, and I recommitted myself to reading it daily. The Ramayana is the sacred story of Sita, Ram, and Hanuman— God in the form of queen, king and perfect servant. It is the epic tale that the Hanuman Chalisa draws from. When we sing the Chalisa, we are tuning our consciousness to this great Lila, the Divine play of God.

During this month, I saw the truth of this first hand. Hanuman permeated my mind, and I began to see him everywhere. Little miracles and synchronicities were sprinkled throughout the day, offering reminders of this deeper Reality I was dipping into. In the final days of that month, I picked up a hitchhiker as I was driving home with the weekly groceries. He noticed the picture of Hanuman on my dashboard and began talking about how much he loved him. It seemed quite serendipitous that he was there, and I took great delight in our conversation. As I dropped him off on the side of the road, he leaned over and looked me directly in the eyes. His voice was intense as he delivered one last parting wisdom.

"You know, they say that when demons see Ram, all they can see is DEATH."

This strange comment, completely out of context from anything else we had discussed, floated awkwardly in the space between us as if not knowing where to land. I was caught off guard and didn't know how to respond, so I simply smiled. But, as I drove away, the comment stayed with me. The moment felt both profound and strange.

Out of all the things he could have said... I thought.

That night I opened up the Ramayana for my nightly bedtime story. I would only read a few pages at a time. Each page is drenched in devotion, and I wanted to ensure I savored every word. Ram and Lakshman were entering the pavilion in Mithila for the bow sacrifice where Ram would prove his worth to marry Sita. The day prior, Ram and Sita saw each other for the first time on earth and fell instantly in love. In truth, They have known each other for eternity. Sita and Rama are not two separate beings. They are the One True Underlying Essence of Reality, known as Lakshmi-Narayana or Sita-Rama. They incarnated on this physical plane in two separate bodies so They could enact Their Lila.

As Ram walked into the pavilion, it's almost as if time stopped. The townspeople were in complete awe as they watched the perfect manifestation of God walk by in His attractive, dark-hued body in perfect proportions. Each person saw in Him the highest manifestation of their own personal desires and ideals "according to the attitude of mind each had towards Him." The citizens saw Him as the pinnacle of humanity. Warriors saw the best warrior. The saints saw His cosmic form with His "many faces, hands, feet, eyes and heads," and the devotees saw Him as "the fountain of all joy."

This list continues, my eyes soaking the wisdom from the page until I was struck with a line I will remember for the rest of my life, right there on page 235 out of 1101. It read, "The DEMONS, who were cunningly disguised as princes, beheld the Lord as DEATH in visible form." (*Sri Ramcharitmanas*, Gita Press).

A satisfying exhale, the kind that softens every muscle and leaves a shimmering wake in every cell, and my mind opened in awe and wonder. This wasn't just a story from some ancient or mythological time. This was a portal into a present Reality that I may never understand, but that I have grown to see as more real and valuable than anything else I will ever know.

These practices are so much more than any temporal experience. It's not about a high or a particular feeling. Of course, this was a *miracle*, and just as fleeting as any emotional high. But, it was pointing me to something deeper than even the excitement of having my mind blown. It hints at the power of the practice and the truth of *relationship*, inviting us into the Lila view, "a realm where everything is God and nothing but God" (Shyamdas[28]).

God has shown me, as They have with generations of devotees from all traditions across the globe, that She is real, that these practices work, and that the lifetimes of sadhana[29] are worth it.

On Chanting Kirtan

They say that these are revealed Names, that ancient Rishis pulled these from the depths of consciousness and placed them in this world as gateways to that Infinite Abode. They say there is something invariably healing about these vibrations, that they melt the ego as they ripple through our being. They say that these Names are perfect forms of God, that the Name and what is Named are one and the same.

All I really know is that these are Names of my Beloved, and by saying them sweetly I partake in the language of the heart, engaging in an eternal love affair. I know that countless devotees have cried their pain, suffering, yearning, and joy into them, a reminder that this love affair is much larger than me. It's as if we are all Gopis partaking in Krishna's dance, each one of us simultaneously claiming Him as our own. I am connected to a tradition of lovers that goes back millennia.

And I know that they *do* work.

Some moments I'm just singing—lost in thoughts or trying to sound pretty—it's as if I don't even remember that the most beautiful gem is coming out of my lips! Other times I'm desperately trying to bring my mind to one point on the Name.

And then there is the softening into It—it's like falling into the Name, as if the Sound Itself is the portal, a sonic river whose current I surrender to as it erodes my separate sense of self.

Other times I am crying out. I am so steeped in my shit, neurosis, and self-hatred that I don't even know where to look or what to do. So I just cry out, and within that intensity the distance is collapsed in an instant.

Other times God is here, I mean, where else could They be? My thoughts, my desires, my emotions, my pain, my confusion, my effort, my shit—it's all

God, and it's beautiful. The most beautiful confusion, the most beautiful thoughts, the most beautiful suffering. And I'm just swimming in it. Swimming in God.

I'm calling out to the Beloved, but who's even calling anyway? The sense of 'me' dissolves in the fiercest and most extravagant melt. We often think of ecstasy as the pinnacle of pleasure, but it's not that; it's the intensity of experience itself, raw in its glory when we stop trying to manage or filter or understand it with the mind; it's the deepest allowance. It's almost too much, but then again what else is there to do but let go?

Until I forget again... I don't know why. Maybe I couldn't handle it, I needed a break, or... it's all just God's dance anyway, and the Beloved has led me back to yearning, or forgetting... but now the yearning and forgetting are a little sweeter. They are prasad, a gift from God to be savored as I dance with my Beloved under the Grace-filled moonlight of devotional song.

Mistaking Planes of Consciousness

There is this place in the woods I would often go to clear my head. It was a short drive and hike to reach my favorite spot, a small clearing with an unassuming tree that I claimed as my own. On this particular day, I sat down in my little forest oasis with an extra-heavy weight. I was pretty lost in life—jobless, aimless and floundering, and this confusion draped over me as an all-consuming depression. I pulled out my pipe and loaded it with some weed. There were no other drugs involved. I sat there after taking the first hit when I heard a rustling in the distance. I looked around but did not see anything. I was about to take my second hit when I heard a giggle. It was a boyish-sounding laugh coming from behind a tree in front of me, maybe about 20 feet away.

I saw a head peak out from behind the tree. The face was green and triangular, and it smiled at me. What... the... fuck...? Stepping out from behind the tree, I shit you not, was a little green elf. It giggled as it took off in a wild sprint towards me, leaping forth from the tree as each step bounced from the mossy forest floor. My jaw unhinged, body in shock, mind racing and not even ready yet to believe my own eyes, the elf jumped into the air and flew towards my face until, get this, it disappeared right into the back of my head. It still lives there, inside of my mind. It talks to me from time to time, and it has never led me astray. It gives me good advice. Life advice. It helps me. It helped me to enroll back in school, start going to the gym, helped me enter a new relationship and get a good job. I don't feel lost any more.

This is one of the more far-out stories I have ever been told, however, it is still one of many. I have had sincere people tell me their experiences involving UFOs, Ascended Masters, Ghosts, Angels, Quija Boards, Sasquatch... you name it. And these were the stories that I believed. I did not have the sense that any of these people were lying, nor that they were confused or delusional. In my own spiritual community, I have heard numerous people tell me they saw and interacted with saint Neem Karoli Baba, a being that left his body in 1973. They were not talking about dreams or visions, but actually seeing and interacting with him in this physical world. I have, of course, had my own set of far-out experiences, which have greatly expanded my own view of reality. It's up to you if you want to believe any of this or not. There are some people who have permanently closed off this door of reality, but for those of us who remain open, what are we to make of this?

I have found it important to have a clear map of the different planes of consciousness. Our maps are how we see the world, and without a proper one, we are going to unconsciously view our experiences from whatever existing maps we already have in place. A person has an encounter with a UFO, and because of their belief in materialism and a predisposition to distrust the government, soon they form an entire paranoid worldview involving physical aliens from other star systems and government suppression of free energy machines. Another person encounters the Holy Spirit in a fundamentalist church. This experience starts a powerful relationship with Christ that turns their life around. They get clean, find a good job and form positive relationships in their community. But, because of the setting of the experience, they are compelled to take on an extremely narrow and rigid view of the world, live in fear of hell, and routinely vote against LGBTQ rights. A now infamous example is when John Lilly, psychonaut and pioneer of the float tank, called the White House after a ketamine trip because of his concerns about an AI takeover.[30]

Situations like these can lead to completely different outcomes if the individuals have a different lens to view them from. Many of the paranoid worldviews I have encountered are formed from a combination of having a non-ordinary experience, an inadequate map, and unfamiliarity with the various planes of consciousness.

Planes of Consciousness

The Vedic worldview utilizes three basic planes[31]—the physical, subtle and causal, although these can be subdivided further.[32] Buddhism, Sufism, and the western esoteric traditions have also written about this in striking similarity.[33]

The physical plane, what we normality think of as reality, is where our physical bodies interact with the world of sensory experience. This is where we exist in our day-to-day waking lives, however, this is really just the outer layer of our experience.

Underneath this lies the subtle plane, which is sometimes called the astral plane. It is always present, but we enter it more deeply when we dream or after the body dies. When we dream, we normally just surf the outer layer, but beneath this there are gradually subtler levels, each one shedding its density like water evaporating to mist until all that's left is the subtlest dance of pure energy. The world's great myths activate these deeper levels and the beings that live there. Just as there are beings in this physical world, the subtle plane is home to various gods, angels, demons and spirit guides.

At an even deeper level is the causal plane. The causal plane is the subtlest of the world of form. It is where the first raw ideas of creation come from, the potential for form and the subtlest of the subtle. On a micro level, it is analogous to our unconscious mind, and we enter it in deep sleep. It is the storehouse of our samskaras, or the deep impressions that shape who we are. On a macro level, this is the seed for all of creation. It is sometimes called Brahma Loka,[34] or the world of Brahma, and when we think of God as creator, this is the place.

There is an even deeper Reality beyond this that words can't adequately describe. It is because of this that the Mandukya Upanishad simply refers to it as "Turiya," or the fourth—the Beyond Beyond. This is God, not as Creator, but as Brahman—pure, undifferentiated, Eternal Consciousness. Sat Chit Ananda. The Ground of Being. This is our innermost Truth, the Atman, the God within. The other planes are associated with sheaths that wrap around the Atman like layers of an onion.[35] In this sense, they are not really separate, but different layers of the same Eternal Consciousness.

These planes influence each other. Most people have at least some understanding of this. For instance, we know that if we have a difficult day it can cause stressful dreams or even nightmares. Likewise, what we spend our time thinking and dreaming about impacts our physical bodies. But this relationship goes even further. There are times when the veils can thin between this world and the next. Through ritual and prayer, we can call upon beings from these other planes, and they can alter our physical reality. This is what we often call a synchronicity or miracle.

Map of Materialism

If we use the map of western materialism, these experiences either won't mean much or we misinterpret them. This is because we see this physical plane as the most important. To the extent that we acknowledge the existence of other realms, we see them as of denigrating validity the further they seem from this physical world. We acknowledge that dreams exist, but we see them as irrelevant. We know that consciousness exists, but we view it as an ephemeral byproduct of the brain. For many of us, it takes some sort of transpersonal experience to shatter this modern myth of materialism.

Through spiritual practice, spontaneous awakening, psychedelics, intuitive insight, or our natural abilities, many of us have encountered beings from other planes. Sometimes we meet them in dreams or visions, and sometimes through more tangible ways such as synchronicities or miracles. There are even times when they can appear in a physical form. With a proper map, we can relate to them in a way that is helpful and in line with reality. However, without one, we are left to either dismiss them as mere hallucinations of the mind, or, if we are unable to due to the intensity of the encounter, we form some pretty awkward worldviews and all-consuming conspiracies to hold our experience.

I am inclined to say that the UFO phenomena are real. At this point, I have read too many case studies and had too many people share their experiences with me to discount it. But I can believe these experiences and allow them to shake my view of reality without necessarily believing in visitations by physical aliens from other star systems. I don't need to believe in a world-government cover up.[36] I don't need to believe in *anything*, however there are maps that exist that have withstood the test of time.

These are much simpler and more coherent than our newer materialistic models. They are able to hold experiences that would otherwise leave us dumbfounded (like when "Italian-looking" space aliens came to Wisconsin in 1961 and brought Joe Simonton a stack of pancakes. He ate one and said it tasted like cardboard. The rest were taken by the FBI for more research.[37]) A good map is not something to blindly cling to, but it can be an indispensable guide when traversing new territory.

If we understand set and setting,[38] we can see why we are not likely to have a vision of Krishna inside of a Christian church. This does not invalidate the existence of Christ or Krishna, but it shows how the doorway colors the light. Jaques Vallee once pondered why medieval Christians were more likely to see angels or demons, Celtic people fairies or elves, and, in our postmodern world, we often see aliens. Carl Jung[39] discussed the timing of the UFO phenomena as coinciding with the rise of the Cold War. This is set and setting on a large, global scale. The setting is today's world of technology and the set is our belief in materialism and the isolation, fear and alienation rampant in our modern world.

But saying that these beings don't have an objective reality in this material plane is not the same as saying they are not real. It would be a mistake to write these off as mere hallucinations of the mind. Like my friend who had an elf jump into the back of his head, there are countless examples of people's lives being changed by beings from other planes. We can't forget the time when the pink light came out of Philip K. Dick's[40] radio and informed him that his son was going to die. If he was a strict materialist and thought he was hallucinating, he would not have been able to convince the doctors to run tests on his seemingly-healthy son, thus saving his life from a rare and deadly disease. My own encounters with non-physical entities have only deepened my faith, offered me healing, and left me more self-secure with a heightened trust in life.

Beyond Materialism

It's common knowledge amongst all faith, mystical, spiritual, folk and Indigenous traditions that there are beings who exist without physical bodies. Some of these beings can help us on our spiritual journeys, alter our physical world and provide us with inspiration, insight and even physical healing. When we have a clear map of consciousness, we can interact with them in a way that furthers our own spiritual evolution.

The subtle realms run on a different set of rules than our physical world. Intuition becomes more important than fact. Fact lives on this objective plane. Here we can run tests, seek agreement, and come to an understanding of the physical laws of the universe. But the subtle planes run on a kind of dream logic. Just as dreams are much more fluid than this physical world, dream logic morphs and flows. The metaphorical meaning of symbols displaces hard logic; insight supersedes cause and effect.

To complicate matters more, this insight has to be filtered through our own personal subjectivity, prey to all of the biases and false perceptions of the human condition. Sometimes we will get insight that resonates, and we feel that we should follow it. Sometimes we will only discover later that what we thought was pure inspiration was really tainted with ego desire. But a proper map, along with the help of wise guides, can help.

Clear direction and guidance is the philosopher's stone that turns errors of judgment into deepened intuition. Every mistake becomes an opportunity to see where we are still caught, where our desires and self-identifications influence and impede our innate discernment. It becomes an opportunity to look within, to probe our mind, understand our personal ticks, attachments and personality structure, and then to reach beyond all of that towards a Greater Inner Truth. And this is the whole point of the journey. If non-physical beings are going to offer us anything, it is an awakening of the Self. Otherwise, it's just another distraction.

Guru Kripa

It is not necessary to meet your guru on the physical plane. The guru is not external.

–Neem Karoli Baba, *Miracle of Love*

For me, the Guru is how God becomes personal. The Guru shows me that God is not just an Eternal, Impartial Truth, or even an All-Pervading Essence of Love, but is also a Being who loves *me* and all of us unconditionally. Before meeting the Guru, I had faith in God, but not a personal relationship. It was the Guru that gave that to me. Now I see that the lines of the Guru Stotram are true: "There is no truth higher than the Guru, no practice higher than the Guru, and no knowledge higher than the Guru."

For some of us the Guru can take the form of a physical person on earth. A true Siddha is said to be a Perfected Master. When you look at Them, all you see is the divine radiance of God shining through. There are no impurities to block the light. This Divine Presence is within all of us as our True Nature, but it is clouded by a web of desire and self-identification. A Siddha has none of that. You can clearly hear the voice of God in Their words, and Their body is a living Murti. Their very life is the wisdom of the Vedas.

Such a Being cannot die. Their physical body may fall away, but the God within was never confined to that body anyway. We can still use Their form to connect with Them. We can look at Their pictures, sing to Them, travel to Their temples, and experience Their Grace through satsang with other devotees. The Guru shows Their devotees that They are still here, often through dreams, synchronicities or miracles, but always through an inner knowing of the heart.

When two or three people gather in my name, I am there.

−Christ (Matt 18:20)

The personal relationship with Christ experienced by many members of the Christian faith could be seen as an example of this. For me and for other members of the Neem Karoli Baba satsang, we refer to our Guru as Maharajji, a Siddha that left His body in 1973. Of course, if we don't feel called to a specific form of the Guru, we can still connect to Them.

The Universal Guru is the God within every heart, and we can connect to Them by reading about any of the saints we are drawn to. Each one is a different mask of God, as if They just swap bodies the way we might change clothes. This analogy took on new meaning for me the day I met Ram Dass for the first time. Still jolted by the Shakti of that encounter, I had a vision that night as I fell asleep on the beach. I saw two figures hovering in front of me—Jesus and Maharajji. They were both levitating a few feet off the ground, and a subtle light illuminated their bodies as they each shapeshifted back and forth into each others' forms. Jesus would turn into Maharajji at the same moment that Maharajji would turn into Christ. This lasted for maybe ten seconds, and then I fell asleep.

Some of us might not require any form. Since the Guru is within, if we are truly quiet, we can hear that Still, Small Voice. The moments when I am connected to my intuitive heart are when I can most clearly see that the Guru guides every step of the journey.

I remember a dream I had shortly before I moved in to live with Ram Dass. Maharajji and I were both in a room together. He was barking ridiculous orders at me, and I was blissfully complying with all of them. "Bend over! Now point one arm up towards the sky! Point the other arm down! Spin in a circle! Now walk backwards!" We both laughed hysterically as my body spun around in the most awkward shape. I woke up from that dream in a state of incomparable joy. The message was clear—Maharajji is the puppet master, I am the puppet, and this dance we enact together is one full of rich, cosmic humor.

Even moments of confusion are the Guru doing His needed work. In suffering I am often ripped away into the deepest surrender. It is these moments that I cling to the Guru, not as a spiritual practice or an exercise in devotion or faith, but out of necessity. Sometimes it feels like hanging on for dear life. Other times it's like I'm completely helpless to do anything, and yet there the Guru is, holding me when I can no longer hold on to anything.

> *You can leave me. I won't leave you. Once I catch hold of you, I don't let go.*
>
> —Neem Karoli Baba, *Miracle of Love*

This is Guru Kripa, or the Grace of the Guru. It is the realization that we are His, that the Guru has us wrapped up in Her warm embrace, that every aspect of our lives serves to draw us towards Them. All we need to do is listen to our heart, and, even when we forget, that too is a part of the Perfection that is the Grace of the Guru. It is through this Grace that we gain faith. This faith is not the same as a belief. Belief is in the mind, but faith is deeper than that. It is a knowing of the heart that the Grace of the Guru is with us every step of the way.

The Problem with Grace

If I were to pick one word that is central to my spiritual worldview, it would be Grace. And yet, I often find it to be the most difficult to talk about. It is profound as Truth and simultaneously problematic as a concept. It is a word that points to the deep nature of Reality and our soul's relationship with God, but any explanation I can possibly think of is problematic if taken literally and applied inappropriately.

For instance, the words, "Everything is Grace," can be either a soothing balm or a dagger to the gut depending on our understanding and application. They can be used to minimize danger, trivialize the suffering of others, or to spiritually bypass our own journey. They can also be that deepest reminder of our inherent OK-ness, even when our body, mind, and life circumstances are not OK. They point us to the indestructible nature of Being, even in the face of death.

Ram Dass has often taught that the words, "Suffering is Grace," are a tool that should only be applied to one's own self. It should never be imposed outwardly on others. This is, of course, good practical advice and a safeguard from becoming an ass, but it also points towards a deeper understanding than the words themselves.

The semanticist Alfred Korzybski coined the now famous phrase, "The map is not the territory." Our ideas about the Universe are not the same as the Universe itself. A map is only useful if it takes us where we want to go. "Suffering is Grace" is one map that can be used to lead us right to the heart, even in the midst of extreme pain, but only in certain circumstances.

This map can also be used to numb our discomfort in witnessing another's pain. Rather than using it to be present with our discomfort, we instead push away and minimize the other's suffering. But Grace is not a concept to minimize pain. It is a force erupting from Infinity that grants us the capacity to hold it.

The concept of grace is like a finger pointing at the moon. Move the hand, and it points us astray.

Sometimes Grace is what we pray for, like a mariner raising their sail and waiting for the winds to come. Other times Grace is more like dusting off an old window to allow in the light of the Sun.

Grace is all-pervading. That means that there is nowhere that Grace does not exist. It is the fabric of Existence itself, and yet... when I think of humanity's worst atrocities and the most traumatic experiences of the human condition, there is no way I can call any of that Grace.

These inconsistencies create a doorway into a space that is deeper than words, where I no longer need to pin concepts to intuitive understanding and where I can truly rest in the spaciousness of Grace.

Spiritually Bypassing "Identity Politics"

It is not our differences that divide us. It is our inability to recognize, accept, and celebrate those differences.

—Audrey Lorde, *Our Dead Behind Us: Poems*

There is a troubling belief gaining traction within the spiritual communities I am a part of. In various ways, people are claiming that so-called "identity politics" further separate us into our individual differences, that somehow they widen the divide of "us and them." I have seen teachings of Ram Dass, MLK, and Neem Karoli Baba used to support this view. This has been almost entirely expressed by white men. Not only is this spiritual bypassing of "identity politics" problematic for the world, but we can't actually be whole until we consider their implications.

Jordan Peterson, a psychologist and professor at the University of Toronto, has gained a following among mostly-white-and-male spiritual seekers. Due to his incorporation of Jungian Psychology, mythology, and transcendence into academic psychological thought, he is often seen as a "spiritual authority" as to why "identity politics" often oversteps its boundaries. In the online video "Jordan Peterson Debunks White Privilege," he states, "I can't quite figure out why the postmodernists have made the canonical distinctions they've made. Race, ethnicity, sexual proclivity, gender identity, those are four dimensions along which people vary, but there is a very large number of dimensions along which people vary... There is an *infinite* number of dimensions along which people vary. So the postmodern question is, why would you privilege some of those distinctions over others?"

Here he is not making any real arguments of merit. He is simply using pseudo-intellectual lines of logic to obfuscate what should be plainly clear: these "distinctions" are four of the primary ways that we discriminate and oppress in our culture.

So-called "identity politics" don't further ensnare us in our separate selves, they actually help free us by shining a light on our deeply embedded identities. For white, heterosexual, cisgender men, our identities are so thoroughly supported and reflected by the dominant culture that they are made invisible to us. The acknowledgment of these identities is often painful because it shows our complicity in an oppressive system. Actually taking the time to understand how white supremacy[41] or patriarchy functions in our culture shows us the ways that they function in our own mind. This does not reify the ego, it only clearly names an underlying structure.

The Buddhist practice of "noting," can be a very powerful tool. Sometimes just naming a complex set of thoughts, emotions, and sensations such as "anger" can have a relieving effect and enable us to gain an objective distance. We can respond to the anger rather than react to it, potentially saving us from causing undue harm to ourselves and others. In this same way, naming white supremacy, patriarchy, heteronormativity, or the gender binary[42] can help us to respond to their influence rather than blindly reacting, thus potentially minimizing their ability to cause harm through our actions.

You are in prison. If you wish to get out of prison, the first thing you must do is realize that you are in prison. If you think you are free, you can't escape.

−G.I. Gurdjieff

For white males, we have a tendency to become defensive about this because it pops the illusion of spiritual progress. It's easy to pretend that we have transcended our egoic identity of race or gender because we have never had to face it as a barrier. So we pretend we have evolved past it rather than acknowledging that we have never even bothered to look. If there was ever a time to use the word "spiritual bypass,"[43] this would be it.

For me, the perennial wisdom of "love everyone and serve everyone" means just that—*everyone*. But we can't even begin to actualize this if we don't acknowledge that not everyone is loved and served by our dominant culture. This includes looking at all of the oppressive structures of our society and working to dismantle them. It means striving to be a good ally. I can't fathom how it means actively working to undermine liberatory movements so those who already hold positions of power can keep their privilege.

And it is true that loving everyone also includes white men. But dismantling white supremacy and patriarchy is not about "hating men" or "hating white people" as some people have claimed. It is a deep recognition that the power imbalance and exploitation in our system is bad for everyone. For instance, bell hooks has written that patriarchy denies men access to "full emotional well-being." She continues to say:

> To truly address male pain and male crisis we must as a nation be willing to expose the harsh reality that patriarchy has damaged men in the past and continues to damage them in the present. If patriarchy were truly rewarding to men, the violence and addiction in family life that is so all-pervasive would not exist.[44]

She continues to say that the crisis facing men has nothing to do with feminism, as many in the men's rights movement believe, but rather is caused by patriarchy, stating:

> The crisis facing men is not the crisis of masculinity, it is the crisis of patriarchal masculinity.

Or as Ram Dass has said, when discussing the ways we deny our complicity in oppressive systems:

> *How much closing of your compassionate heart must it take to continue to play the game of king of the mountain, what's in it for me?... The pain for all of you is that we are not living our life in harmony with our deepest wisdom. And that is my pain... My heart says there is justice. My heart says there is compassion. Because that is what my heart is, it's a just and compassionate entity. And so is yours. And we armor them with rationalization to deal with the fact that we are acting in ways that are not just and are not compassionate.*[45]

Like any addiction, the benefits gained from an oppressive system are only masks that cover a deep spiritual pain. The defensiveness we feel about acknowledging this covers the fear that we aren't strong enough to face these inner demons. We have never been fulfilled by this system. Just as Trump points to a past that never existed by saying he will "Make America great again," the men's rights movement and other reactionaries such as Jordan Peterson point to a mythical time when white men were actually deeply fulfilled.

If we want to actually think freely, we need to actively work to decondition our mind from our cultural programming. If we want to be free from the limits of identity, we need to acknowledge all of the ways that identity functions in our life. If we want to stop labeling other people as "them," we need to first understand who we have already labeled that way.

Rather than spiritually bypassing "identity politics," let's actually work to acknowledge our "imperialist, white supremacist, capitalist, patriarchy"[46] and all of the ways it has infiltrated our mind.

Bracing Against the World

Our samskaras,[47] or the accumulation of habits formed from past action and thought, are deep impressions that have dug themselves into our mind-body system. These samskaras manifest in the form of bracing.[48] We tighten in our mind-body in order to push away unpleasantness or to grab at the desirable. It is this contraction that creates the illusion of separation. By bringing our awareness to these deep holdings, they begin to loosen on their own, returning to their natural state. We stop bracing against the world.

I usually hear this teaching applied to our personal lives. We brace against our relationships to other people, to work, and to ourselves. But, there is another set of deep contractions that we rarely, if ever, talk about.

We constantly brace against the immense suffering that surrounds us and the inevitable guilt we feel as an accomplice. Every time we buy something... *anything*, drive a car, turn on the electricity in our homes, or even travel to a dharma retreat, our mind-body braces against the horror of our involvement in the exploitation of people and the planet, and we brace again to stave off the helplessness of having no escape in sight. It is this bracing that allows us to continue without fully acknowledging our role as accomplice, or if we do it stays hidden from sight or subdued as a subtle whisper.

We brace out of the mistaken fear that we will drown in the world's pain, but what we seek to protect is merely the outer shell of our Being. By protecting it, we not only create a dam from the world, but also from ourselves. The world's suffering *is* our suffering. We spend precious energy maintaining this illusion of separation.

When we lower the floodgates, this outer shell begins to crumble against life's oncoming river. What remains is something remarkable—the fierce courage of an open heart. This heart carries the tides of grief and beauty on its inhale and exhale like a billowing sea, informing the way we inhabit the world and animating each step. This heart sings the song of the world.

For most of us, this is not a one-time event, but a continual and gradual letting go. Each time I allow myself to feel, I discover a new part of me that is still holding on, not yet ready to let go, still believing in a *someone* to protect from a world *out there.*

But this also leaves me with a strengthened faith in the process, for an open heart is inherently satisfying. It teaches that the world's pain contains seeds of its power. And, if we are ever going to change the oppressive power structures at play, we will need that power to do so.

Problems cannot be solved without being acknowledged, and all of us, whether we have spent years in spiritual retreat or years protesting on the streets, can go a little deeper.

Spirituality Does Not Need Pseudoscience

The Ground of Being does not require science for its proof. It does not require quantum physics. Once tasted, it can never fully leave us, and no amount of evidence could ever disprove it. Once we see that we are the depth of Eternal Consciousness, then every thought, sensation, experience, and even the sense of "I" become mere clouds passing through the Vast Sky of Being. We still may become lost in the clouds, but we know in our hearts that the sky is there.

Once this awakens, God's handiwork is seen everywhere, including in science. There, at the quantum level, at the edge of the Universe, or at the beginning of time, it seems we see the first dance of formlessness into form, where the Great Mystery flirts with our rational mind, turning over our assumptions of reality and opening us up like a Zen koan.

But it would be a mistake to look for proof in this. There is no mathematical or scientific proof for God, and trying to place one where it does not exist leads to pseudoscience. This is the mistake of many New Age thinkers today. They see the miracle of the One sprinkled throughout the many, and they wish to share this with others. Many are sincere in their efforts, but nonetheless they actually widen the gap between spirituality and science by pushing away those with little patience for shoddy logic.

But if instead of looking for proof we look for poetry, then the dance of creation can delight us with each quark, black hole, and quantum superposition, awakening us to our True Nature. The Universe, too, is just a cloud passing through the Sky of Being, and awe and wonder are the steps towards that Great Stillness within.

Faith and Suffering

I love suffering. It brings me so close to God. –Neem Karoli Baba

These words are often my lifeline when it feels like I can't breathe. When the constriction of mind cuts me off from the world, and when I am unable to connect with anything or anyone outside of myself, these words remind me to relax into my suffering and arrive at its unmistakable truth—that God is here, in this moment, in *this* suffering.

The suffering is still here, but now there is nowhere else I would rather be. There is a space around it. There is room to breathe.

In these moments I've found that true joy can coexist with suffering. An unbearable Love can be found within even the most horrendous agony. I'm often awestruck by the unexpected arising of gratitude. I become thankful for this unasked-for pain and for losing my balance enough to catapult me into a deeper stillness.

It reminds me why I am on this path and why I do these practices. I don't write for people to read, I don't sing for people to listen, I don't meditate to be calm, and I don't pray for some reward. I may believe that tomorrow or even in a few moments, but for now... this is the gift, here, in this erratic pain.

This strengthens my faith. It becomes evident that, even when I forget and mistakenly try to stroke my ego or fulfill my desires, it does its silent work. Through singing the Names, through looking at my Guru, through service, and through prayer, Grace shines Its holy fire on the rope of my narcissism and cinders its threads even as I work to tie knots.

I have faith that I will be brought back to this Truth, again and again, even through pain as long as it's needed, for once its fire has burnt the last thread, there will be no more rope or the tying of knots.

Death of a Teacher

Below is what I wrote the night I learned Ram Dass left his body. Writing is one of my main ways that I work through grief, and crafting these words was incredibly healing. Since then, I did go to Maui, and I got to touch his feet. I will forever have burned in my mind the power and beauty of staying up through the night in satsang, doing puja, singing bhajan, and performing aarti to his body as it lay covered in flowers in the early morning hours before sunrise.

What makes Ram Dass's life truly remarkable is the way he showed us what is possible when we fully honor our human hearts. Ram Dass died into love, reaching the state of what the Narada Bhakti Sutras call "Parama Prem;" it's the full ripening of Bhakti, a softening into that Supreme and Eternal Love. And yet, Ram Dass died as a human being, just like you and me. He never once pretended to be anything other than human. He lived and died in a way that shows that spiritual liberation is found, not despite our humanity, but because of it. To me, his deepest teaching is that "Loving Awareness" is truly accessible to us all. It is our birthright.

I have come to find that I actually feel Ram Dass's presence more now than ever before. It's like a valve has been released in my heart that I never knew existed, and this vast oceanic Love can come pouring in.

I now feel the words I wrote that night to be a true reality: "His own teachings point the way to stay in union with him. He is merged in Love, and that Love is always present." Ram Dass is here, now, and available for any of us searching wisdom, guidance, or the depths of Love Itself.

December 23rd, 12:09 am

Ram Dass has left his body and merged with Neem Karoli Baba, dissolved in the ocean of Love.

I feel the waves of grief, and I love each wave. But more than anything my heart just feels full. His own teachings point the way to stay in union with him. He is merged in Love, and that Love is always present.

I was supposed to go see him on January 23rd. My schedule is pretty busy, so I was grateful I could carve out a few days to be in his presence. And now he's gone.

"Well, I guess I won't get to have that one last grand moment with him," I thought. All of the fantasies I had about how it would be like when I saw him played through my mind. This was followed by, "That's just an attachment." And then it became just another thought, and I loved the thought, just for existing.

Then came the next thought: "Ram Dass taught me how to do that."

Ram Dass has completely changed the way I think, the way I relate to my experiences, how I fill my time, where I place my value... My life can never be the same because of one man. I might get caught up in mundane matters and avoid my daily practices, but his influence is always present as a constant backdrop. It touches every single aspect of my life, and there are no words to describe the kind of gratitude that comes from that. None.

I owe him more than I can ever repay, and that is one of the ways that a true teacher shows us what Grace is.

There are so many stories flooding my awareness right now, but I will share this one. There were 20 of us in the pool doing a Q&A with Ram Dass. A person asked, "I have been thinking a lot about how everything is always changing. And so I am wondering, what is the difference between loss and change?"

Usually when a question was asked of him, there was that long pause, as if the question was answered by the silence first so his words could validate it after. But in that moment, it was in reverse. Ram Dass spoke before she even finished her sentence. A single word, razor sharp, leaving behind a searing wake of silence.

"Attachment," he said.

When I saw Ram Dass in Taos for the Grand Opening of the new Hanuman Temple, there was one night where I couldn't sleep, and so I wrote him a handwritten letter. In it I admitted something that I was too timid to ever say to his face. "In my heart of hearts, you are no different to me than Neem Karoli Baba."

And it's true. It's true now more than ever, but it's always been true.

Ram Dass, I never had the nerve to bow down to touch your feet. I always wanted to, but I saw the way you recoiled when people reached out for them. I knew you never wanted that. Instead, you pointed us to Neem Karoli Baba, known to us as Maharajji.

You always said that Maharajji lives in your imagination. So too, you both live in mine. Tonight, I bow to touch your holy, precious feet in my mind.

ENDNOTES AND APPENDIX

Endnotes

p. 7   [1]   The now famous story of how Ram Dass, Krishna Das, Danny Goleman, Rameshwar Das and others were on a bus together in India trying to find Neem Karoli Baba, known as Maharajji. Somehow he knew where they were going to be before they even knew where they were going.

p. 8   [2]   Maharajji is talked about in this book the most in depth in the chapter, "Guru Kripa." To learn more about this great saint and Siddha, I highly recommend Ram Dass's *Miracle of Love* and Dada Mukerjee's *By His Grace.*

p. 8   [3]   Dassi Ma now runs Hanuman Maui, Ram Dass Loving Awareness Sanctuary with Stever Dallman on Maui, fulfilling the dream of many who have set foot in Ram Dass's home and felt the palpable sense of the Sacred.

p. 11   [4]   A service and kirtan group dedicated to lowering the barriers to access spiritual teachings and practices. Learn more at www.kripa.guru

p. 11   [5]   *Franny and Zoey*

p. 11   [6]   Verse 4:24—translation from Winthrop Sargeant

p. 11   [7] Brahman is one of the many names for God in India.
It specifically refers to God in the impersonal, absolute,
universal, transcendent (and imminent), and ineffable
aspect. There can be no image or description for Brahman.
The word serves to remind us that we can never contain God
in our mind.

p. 12   [8] Mahārājji means "great king" and is a term of endearment
that is common in India.

p. 13   [9] Siddha means "perfected being" and is explained more
fully in the chapter "Guru Kripa."

p. 13   [10] International Alphabet of Sanskrit Transliteration

p. 13   [11] Saṃskṛta—a "perfected work." It consists of saṃ
(together, good, well, perfected) and kṛta (made, formed,
work).

p. 14   [12] Lakṣhmī

p. 14   [13] Nārāyaṇa

p. 15   [14] As a cisgender man, I am following the lead of queer
spiritual activists in this. Both in India and around the world,
activists are freeing our concept of God from limited, binary
thinking. Although many scholars and activists have written
about this, maybe it was most succinctly stated by Janelle
Monae when she said, "God is nonbinary."

p. 45   [15]   Bhakti is "the nature of supreme love of God" (Narada Bhakti Sutras, verse 2).

p. 48   [16]   From: *Miracle of Love: Stories about Neem Karoli Baba*, Ram Dass

p. 53   [17]   See chapter: "Beliefs Masquerading as Truth" (page 49)

p. 58   [18]   Satsang is derived from Sanskrit satsangha, which comes from *sat* (true) and *sangha* (association/company). It is the spiritual association surrounding Truth.

p. 60   [19]   Bhagavad Gītā—*Song of God*. Gītā means song, and Bhagavat is a name of God that literally means "full or splendour" or "holy." The root bhaj, which means "adore" or "worship," becomes "bhaga," meaning good fortune, majesty, beauty, or loveliness. The Viṣṇu Purāṇa states that Bhaga indicates the six properties of "dominion, might, glory, splendour, wisdom, and dispassion." The suffix "vat," gives a sense of possession, so a Bhagavān is a Being who possesses Bhaga. According to the Viṣṇu Purāṇa, "That essence of the supreme is defined by the term Bhagavat: the word Bhagavat is the denomination of that primeval and eternal God: and he who fully understands the meaning of that expression, is possessed of holy wisdom, the sum and substance of the three Vedas" (VI., translation by Wilson).

p. 60   [20]   Translation based on multiple sources, especially the work by Winthrop Sargeant

p. 61   [21]   Dharma—from the root Dhr- to hold, maintain. It is a complex word that can mean cosmic law, one's nature, virtue, right conduct, purpose, duty, and religion. There is no one word in English for this term, however the closest I have ever heard is from Keshav Kishor Sharan, head of the Braj Mandir in Holbrook, MA, who said, "Dharma means relationship." www.sriradhabhakti.org

p. 61   [22]   Indigenous, Black, PoC, people from the Global South, and those experiencing poverty will be the ones most harmed, and these are also the groups that have contributed the least to global climate change. It is for this reason that many activists are calling for climate reparations. If it is too late to stop the effects, then those who contributed and benefited the most from the causes of climate change have a responsibility to pay for the damage caused to those who will be the most harmed.

p. 62   [23]   See: Global Assessment Report on Biodiversity and Ecosystem Services by the United Nations, 2019

p. 62   [24]   "Something Braver Than Trying to Save the World," *Moral Ground*, Moore & Nelson

p. 64   [25]   Carl Rogers is considered one of the founders of humanistic psychology. His concept of "unconditional positive regard" is still considered to be a crucial element of any healing relationship.

p. 64   26   Dominant culture (white supremacy, patriarchy, colonialism, upper-and-middle classism) upholds its ideology, worldview, and values through discourse. According to Foucault, "Discourses are more than ways of thinking and producing meaning. They constitute the 'nature' of the body, unconscious and conscious mind and emotional life of the subjects they seek to govern" (Weedon, 1987, p. 108).

p. 71   27   The Hanuman Chalisa is a 40-verse prayer to Lord Hanuman. Hanuman is said to be the embodiment of perfect devotion and selfless service. He is the place in our Being that IS Love and Service. He is also the Grace that opens us up to this vast expanse of Love within. The Chalisa is an invocation that opens our hearts to Hanuman's Grace.

p. 74   28   From: *Ecstatic Couplets*, 2010

p. 74   29   Sādhana—refers to one's spiritual practice. It comes frrom the root sādh, "accomplish, effect, bring about," and literally means any activity that brings about a desired goal. A sādhak is someone who is on the spiritual path but still has work to do. Another related term, sādhu, or "holy person," is someone who is solely focused on practicing sādhana. Both of these terms are different from a Siddha, or "perfected being," one who has already fully accomplished the goal of Sādhana.

p. 78   [30]   This is well documented, but one notable book describing this is Erik Davis's *High Weirdness: Drugs, Esoterica, and Visionary Experience in the Seventies*

p. 79   [31]   Plane is a term that comes from the modern, western esoteric movement. It was first coined by the neoplatonic philosopher, Proclus Lycaeus, and became popular in the 20th century due to Theosophy. However, we don't have a good term in English to explain the bodies, states of consciousness, and lokas from Vedic thought. "Planes of consciousness" is as close as I can find. It is also a term used by Ram Dass as well as several prominent teachers from the 20th century including Shivananda, Yogananda, and Meher Baba.

p. 79   [32]   See: Sarira Traya for the three bodies, Mandukya Upanishad for the 4 planes of consciousness, Taittiriya Upanishad for the 5 sheaths, and Vishnu Purana for the 14 lokas

p. 79   [33]   There are of course notable differences between these systems, and this statement is not meant to water down the beautiful differences between the world's spiritual and mystical traditions, but only to point out that they are similar enough to suggest a sense of universality.

p. 80   [34]   Also known as Satya Loka, and it is said to be the home of Brahma, or the God of Creation

p. 80   [35]   See: Taittiriya Upanishad

p. 81   [36]   To be clear, I am well aware of credible reports from government officials with security clearances that say there is physical evidence of UFOs that has been collected by the U.S. government. For me, this evidence takes me further into the state of not knowing. But even if we were to receive total proof of alien life, it wouldn't change the stance of this essay. For more on this, here are a few recent articles: https://www.nytimes.com/2020/07/23/us/politics/pentagon-ufo-harry-reid-navy.html https://www.nytimes.com/2020/07/28/insider/UFO-reporting.html

p. 81   [37]   See: Jacque Vallee's *Passport to Magonia*

p. 81   [38]   "Set" refers to mindset, and setting is the physical space. The terms were first coined by Timothy Leary for traversing psychedelic landscapes, however it applies to any transpersonal experience.

p. 82   [39]   See: *Flying Saucers: A Modern Myth of Things Seen in the Skies*

p. 82   [40]   See: *Valis*

p. 90 [41] Legal scholar Francis Lee Ansley defines white supremacy as the "political, economic and cultural system in which whites overwhelmingly control power and material resources, conscious and unconscious ideas of white superiority and entitlement are widespread, and relations of white dominance and non-white subordination are daily reenacted across a broad array of institutions and social settings." It is central to the field of critical race theory and explained in detail by scholars such as Derek Bell and bell hooks. As Vann Newkirk II writes in his Atlantic article, "What is White Supremacy," this definition is also supported by well-known activists and thinkers such as James Baldwin and Martin Luther King Jr.

p. 90 [42] See: Judith Butler, "Gender Trouble: Feminism and the Subversion of Identity"

p. 91 [43] Coined by John Welwood as the "tendency to use spiritual ideas and practices to sidestep or avoid facing unresolved emotional issues, psychological wounds, and unfinished developmental tasks." It is often used by those with unearned privilege as a tactic to uphold power and overlook the deep pain caused by the oppressive systems that keep that privilege in place.

p. 91 [44] bell hooks, *The Will to Change, Men, Masculinity, and Love*

p. 92   [45]   From: Ram Dass's 1995 Lecture "The Advanced Class"

p. 92   [46]   A term coined by bell hooks to describe "the interlocking systems of domination that define our reality"

p. 93   [47]   Saṃskāra—has the same roots as Saṃskṛta, but here refers to mental impressions

p. 93   [48]   I first learned of the term *bracing* from Will Johnson, author of *Breathing through the Whole Body* and *The Posture of Meditation.*

Sanskrit Pronunciation Guide

VOWELS

- a -as in c<u>u</u>t

- ā -as in t<u>a</u>ll

- i -as in b<u>i</u>t

- ī -as in b<u>ee</u>t

- u -as in p<u>u</u>t or f<u>oo</u>t

- ū -as in br<u>u</u>te or c<u>u</u>te

- e -as in b<u>ay</u> or h<u>ey</u>

- ai -as in s<u>i</u>gh or b<u>i</u>cycle

- o -as in h<u>o</u>pe

- au -as in s<u>ou</u>nd

- ṛ -as in cu<u>rl</u> (the tongue curls back to the retroflex position at the alveolar ridge

CONSONANTS

- v is a little softer, close to <u>w</u>

- ś (palatal) as in <u>sh</u>ame

- ṣ (retroflex) similar to di<u>sh</u>

- c always soft as in <u>ch</u>urch

- ṅ (velar/guttural) like su<u>ng</u>

- ñ (palatal) as in ca<u>n</u>yon

- ṇ (retroflex) like re<u>n</u>own

- -ṃ -as in cal<u>m</u>

- ḥ -softly echoes the preceding vowel with a puff of air. So namaḥ would be "namaha"

ASPIRATED CONSONANTS (kh, gh, ch, jh, th, dh, ph, bh) The h's are pronounced so that- "th" is pronounced like hothouse, not as in theatre. Goddess Rādhā, for instance, is sounded "Rād-hā."

1 LIPS/ LABIAL CONSONANTS (p ph b bh m) These are sounded the same as in English. They are sounded with the lips.

2 TEETH/ DENTAL CONSONANTS (t th d dh n) Pronounced with the tongue touching the back of the teeth. In English our tongue is often on the gum behind the teeth, making our dental stops sound like something between a true dental and a retroflex.

3 CEREBRAL/RETROFLEX CONSONANTS (ṭa ṭha ḍa ḍha ṇa) The tongue is curled back to touch the alveolar ridge. (See figure 3.)

4 PALATALS (c ch j jh ñ) These are sounded similar to their English counterparts (ca is a soft c as in "church"). You will notice that the tongue flattens at the roof of the mouth when you sound a ja or ca sound. The 'ñ' sound does the same. When you say the word "nya," you are getting a sense of the 'ñ' sound. You will notice that the tongue flattens in a similar way as it does when you say "ja."

5 GUTTURALS (k kh g gh ṅ) These are sounded similar to their English counterparts. They feel like they are coming from the back of the throat and are sounded by the back of the tongue touching the throat. The 'ṅ' is sounded by completely closing off the back of the throat with the tongue. This happens naturally when you say "ing."

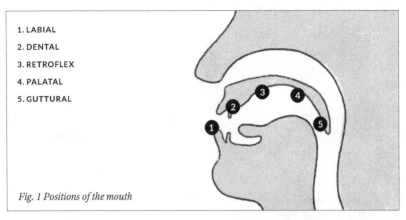

1. LABIAL
2. DENTAL
3. RETROFLEX
4. PALATAL
5. GUTTURAL

Fig. 1 Positions of the mouth

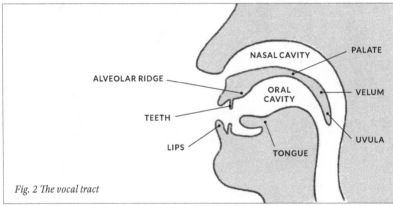

NASAL CAVITY

PALATE

ALVEOLAR RIDGE

ORAL CAVITY

VELUM

TEETH

LIPS

TONGUE

UVULA

Fig. 2 The vocal tract

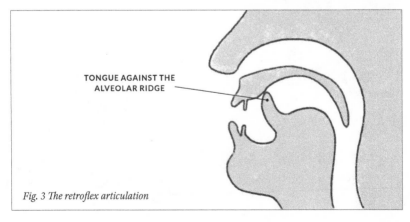

TONGUE AGAINST THE ALVEOLAR RIDGE

Fig. 3 The retroflex articulation

Vedic Maps of Consciousness

Terms used in this book	4 STATES OF CONSCIOUSNESS Mandukya Upanishad	BEINGS IN EACH REALM Puranas
PHYSICAL PLANE	WAKING Jāgṛt-avasthā	EMBODIED SOULS
SUBTLE PLANE	DREAMING Svapna-avasthā	DEMONS GHOSTS CELESTIAL BEINGS ANGELS GODS SIDDHAS RISHIS
CAUSAL PLANE	DEEP SLEEP Suṣupti-avasthā	GOD AS CREATOR, SUSTAINER, AND DESTROYER
	4TH STATE Turiya *Beyond the Beyond*	NIRGUNA BRAHMAN God without attributes

| 5 SHEATHS | 3 BODIES |
| Taittriya Upanishad | Sharira Traya |

FOOD SHEATH Annamaya kosha *Physical body*	**GROSS BODY** Sthula Śarīra
VITAL SHEATH Pranamaya kosha *Prana,* or *energy body*	
MENTAL SHEATH Manomaya kosha *Manas,* or *surface mind*	**SUBTLE BODY** Sūkṣma Śarīra or *Linga śarīra*
INTELLECT SHEATH Vijnanamaya kosha *Buddhi,* or *intuitive intellect*	
BLISS SHEATH Anandamaya kosha *Chitta,* or *storage of past impressions*	**CAUSAL BODY** Karana Śarīra

ATMAN
The Self

ABOUT THE AUTHOR

Sitaram Dass (K. Sandin) spent several years serving his beloved teacher Ram Dass on Maui, where he was shown the path of Bhakti Yoga, the yoga of service and devotion to God. Through writings, music, teachings, workshops, and one-on-one counseling, he works to strengthen our sense of the Timeless Sacred in today's modern and fast-paced world.

He draws his inspiration from his beloved teacher Ram Dass, the great Indian Saint Neem Karoli Baba, Hanuman, and the Divine Mother. He also finds inspiration in all of the world's great wisdom and mystic traditions and has received great benefit, insight, and grace from Sufism, Buddhism, Hermeticism, Christianity, and modern psychotherapy.

He is a member of Kripa, a purpose-driven kirtan group committed to the wide accessibility of kirtan and Bhakti Yoga. Kripa works to lower the barriers of access to contemplative and devotional practices through affordable, free, and donation-based offerings and prison outreach. Learn more about their important work at: https://kripa.guru

He lives with his life partner, Jamie, and their cats, Prem and Olive, in the redwoods of Northern California.

CPSIA information can be obtained
at www.ICGtesting.com
Printed in the USA
LVHW110716090421
683977LV00006B/99